Welcome to......
Country Girl Corner

Lesley De Matos

Country Girl Corner Publishing

First published in the United Kingdom by:
Country Girl Corner Publishing
'Rockville' 10 Plaines Close, Cippenham,
Berkshire SL1 5TY

ISBN: 978-0-9576044-0-7

This book can be ordered from:
info@countrygirlcorner.co.uk
www@countrygirlcorner.co.uk

A CIP catalogue record for this book is
available from The British Library

Copyright © Country Girl Corner 2013

All rights reserved. No part of this book
can be reproduced or transmitted in any
form or by any means electronic or mechanical
including photocopying, recording or by
any information retrieval system without
written permission of the publisher.

Although every precaution has been taken in
the preparation of this book the author
and publisher assume no responsibility
for errors or omissions, neither is any
liability assumed for damages resulting from
the use of the information contained herein.

All rights reserved

My thanks to Danny and Lucia who get dragged around to shops and shows to look at 'pretty things' and for putting up with the house looking like a workshop as I take over every flat surface.

For Granny Annie who would make my favourite dinner, teach me how to crochet 'granny squares', pull the settee closer to the TV to watch Muhammad Ali and then later tuck me up in bed under her feather eiderdown.

For my Mum, who would smile and look despairingly at me when I would be lying on the floor on top of newly acquired fabric with the scissors in my hand, and ask 'what are you making' only to be told 'trousers' as if it was the most natural thing in the world.

For my Dad who makes every conversation into a lesson, every object into a 'craft design and technology' topic and from whom I've learnt that dressmaking is the same as woodwork - only with fabric.

To my other friends I've met along the way who have helped and supported, chatted and discussed, shared the interest and encouraged the obsession.

many thanks

Lesley

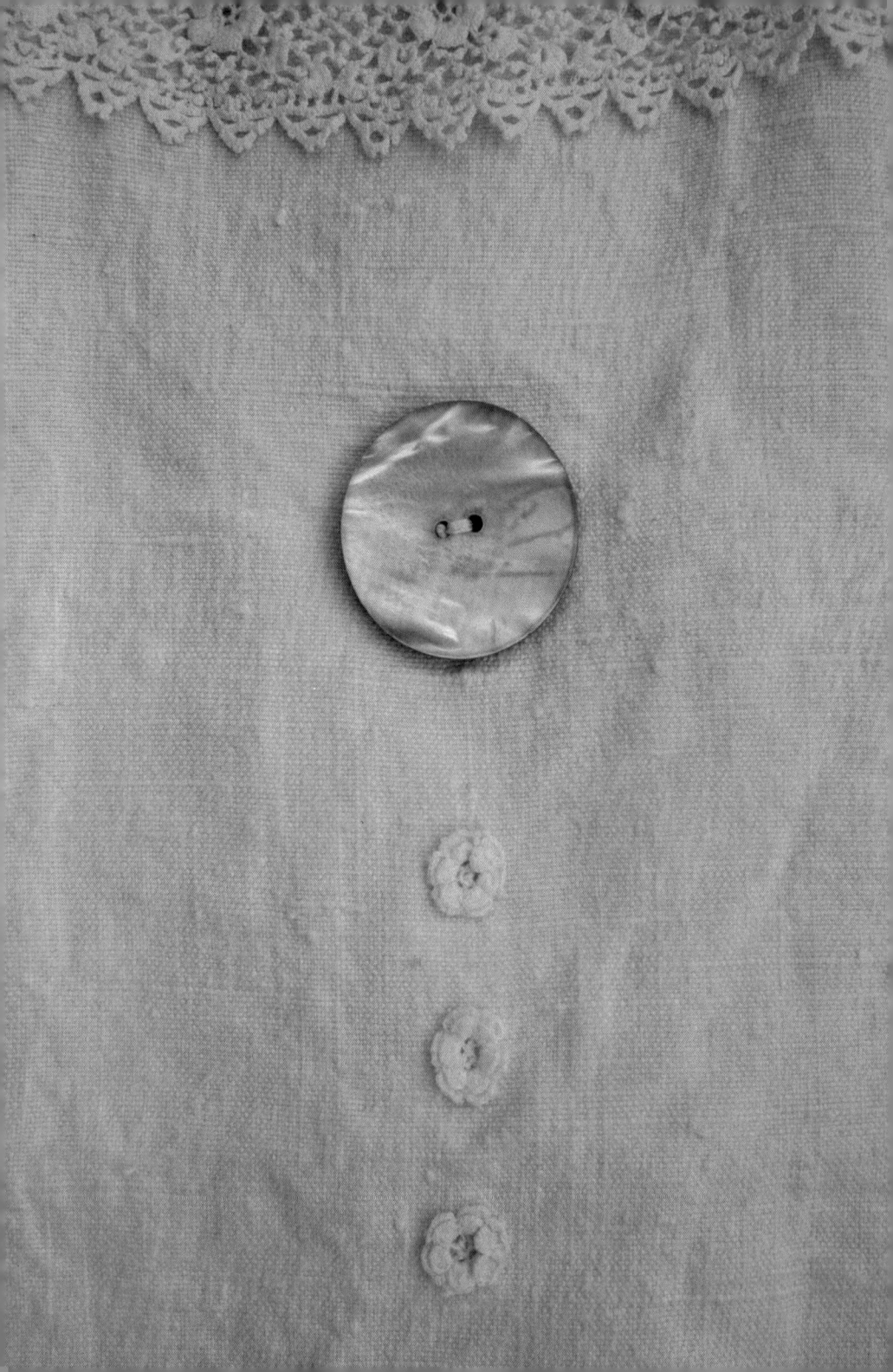

I was taught to type while I was at school, we would
go once a week on the bus to the college and would
have a coffee in town before class. They had manual
typewriters at the time and if you were one of the
last ones into the class you would have to sit at the
machines which had no letters on the keys (these
were to teach you to touch type and you couldn't
look at the letters as you typed)
Things have obviously moved on since then, and
having had the idea to put together all my
patterns in a book I needed to get to grips with
Photoshop. So armed with the basics achieved
purely on a 'need to know' basis, I have put all
this together, so it may not be perfect, may not
line up exactly, the letters may not all be the
right size, but it just shows you, what can
be achieved with a little bit of knowledge and
a very big obsession.

my pin-cushion..........

Country Girl Corner

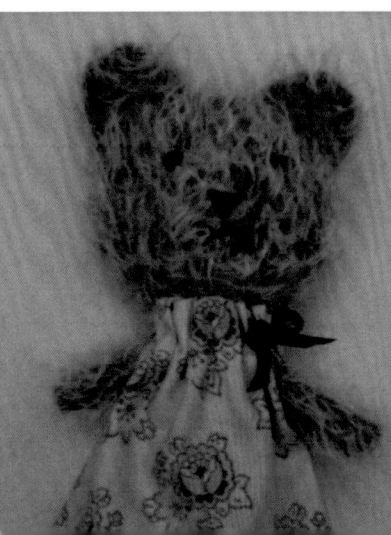

www.CountryGirlCorner.co.uk

Missy
(Lavender cat)

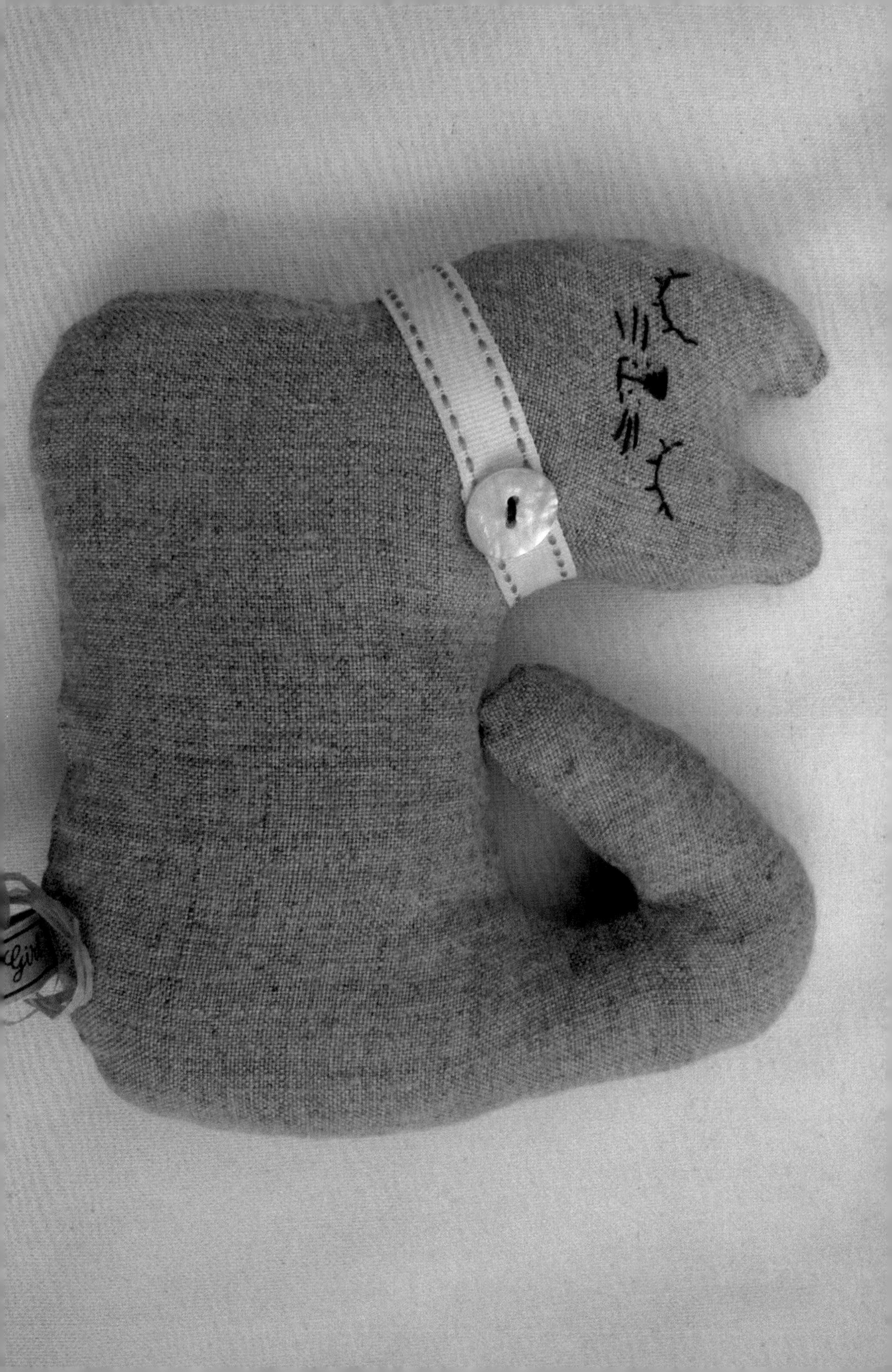

Missy

You will need:

Fabric 40 x 25 cm (16" x 10")
Toy filler
Embroidery Thread (brown)
Contrasting ribbon
handful of dried lavender (optional)

Trace around the pattern piece and pin pattern to double layer of fabric (right sides facing)
Don't sew over the 'leave open' part of pattern. Sew around the edge of the pattern, trim 1cm (1/2") around the pattern piece, remove pattern, snip into curves and turn to right side out
Fill with toy filler (more filler will make a more solid toy, less filler will make it more huggable) Fill the centre of the tummy with a handful of lavender and then tuck in the raw edges and sew across.
Take a pencil and lightly draw on the face, and then with the embroidery thread sew a back stitch along the lines
It doesn't matter if your lines aren't very straight because this will bring more character to your toy
Tie your chosen ribbon around the cat's neck and tie in a bow
or sew on a button to fasten

'Blue' with 'Blue'
(he didn't last long....)

Buttons
(the cute dog)
and the little kittens

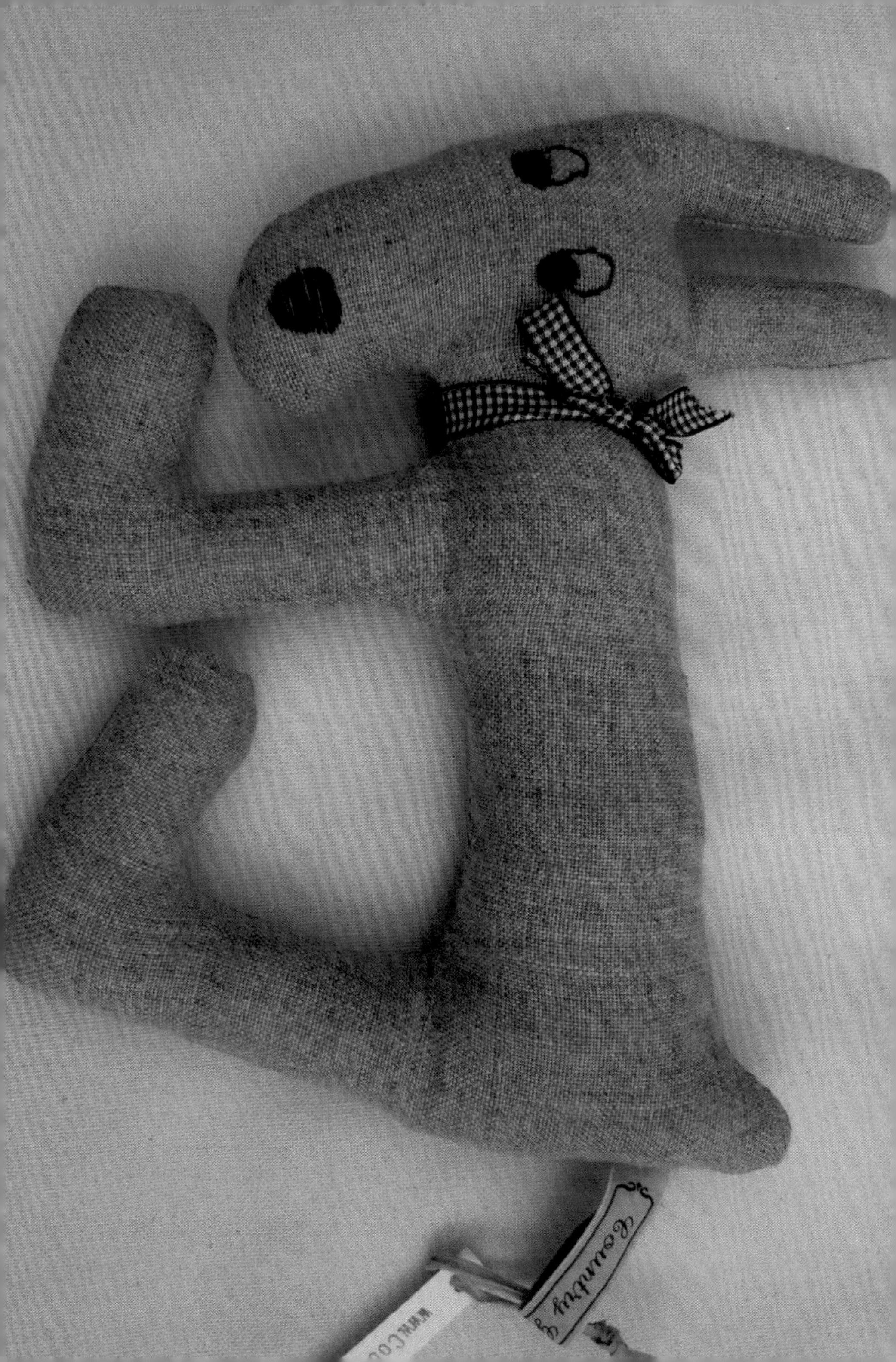
Country

Buttons (the cute dog) and little kittens

The dog and the little kittens are all made using the same basic principal as for Missy the lavender cat.

Trace the pattern and cut it out, pin to a double layer of fabric (right sides together)
Sew around the edge of the pattern (leaving the gap open where indicated)
Cut 1cm (1/2") around the pattern shape
remove the pattern, snip into the curves, turn piece through to the right side and stuff,
slip stitch over the opening
sew on the face features

For the little kittens, take a piece of string approx 10cm (4") and tie a knot in each end. Tuck one knot in the opening and sew across (having the extra knot in there prevents the tail slipping out)

Tie a ribbon around the neck (I usually add a little bell on the kittens)

Give them a name and you're done

I made these based on the Town cat and the Country cat. The Town cat is made with linen and has a lovely red ribbon collar, and the Country Cat is made with tea-dyed calico and and has a rough string collar

Hop & Lavender bags (see page 53)

All friends together...

Quilt in a Day

A number of years ago, I had seen an advert for a 'quilt in a day' and armed with a bag of fabric, I joined the class in a church hall near the patchwork shop in Hampton Court. I had never used a rotary cutter, mat and ruler to cut my fabric before (I had only ever cut my fabric with scissors!) So, the whole day was full of firsts......I kept up with the teacher, kept sewing, concentrated and sure enough at the end of the day, I turned my quilt, sewed up the edge and was quite amazed that I had made a 'quilt in a day'

What I then realised was that only a few people had actually made their quilt and most went home with their bag of bits, so I advertised that I could take this bag of good intentions and turn it into a lovely quilt as intended

xxx

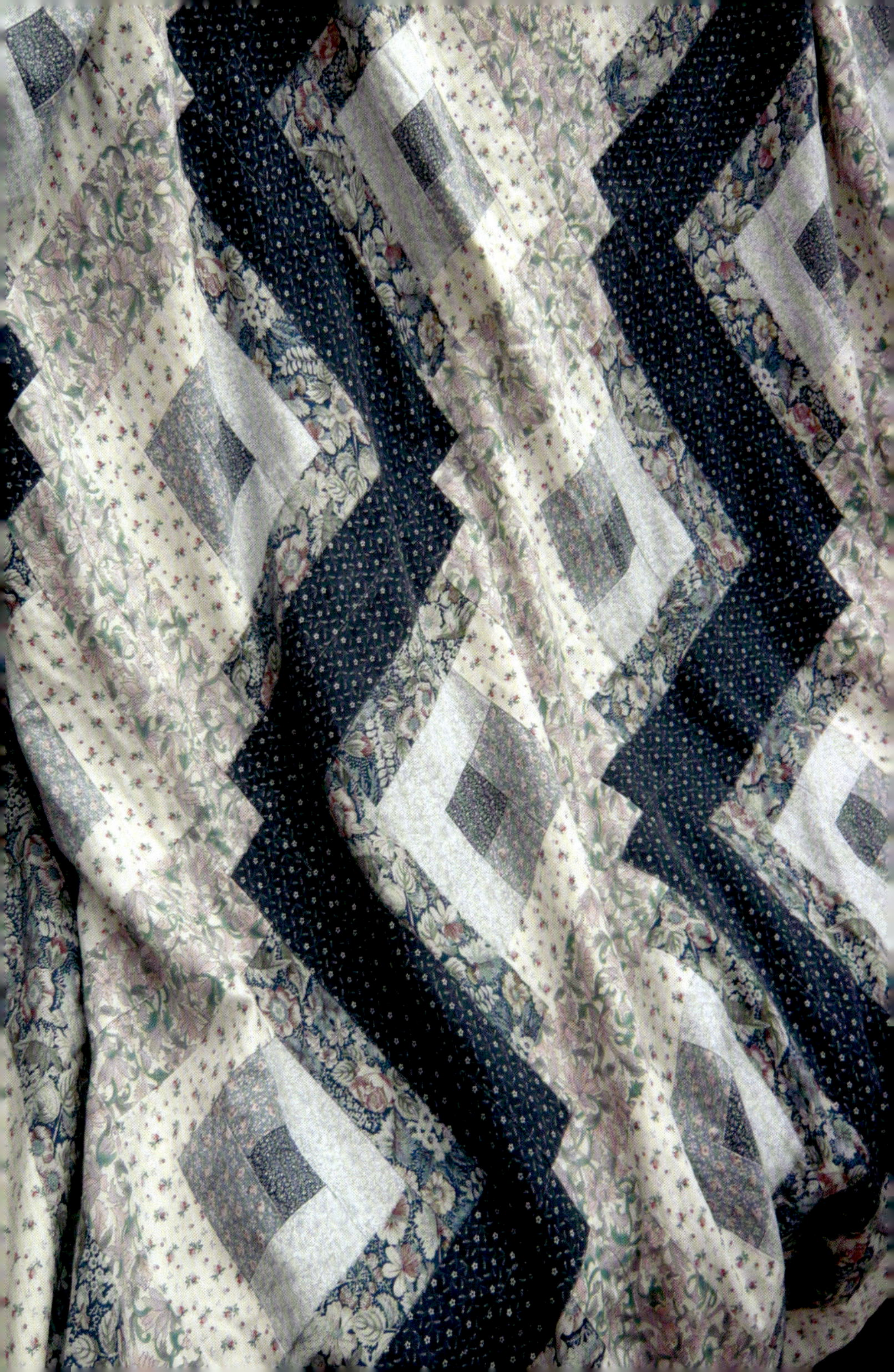

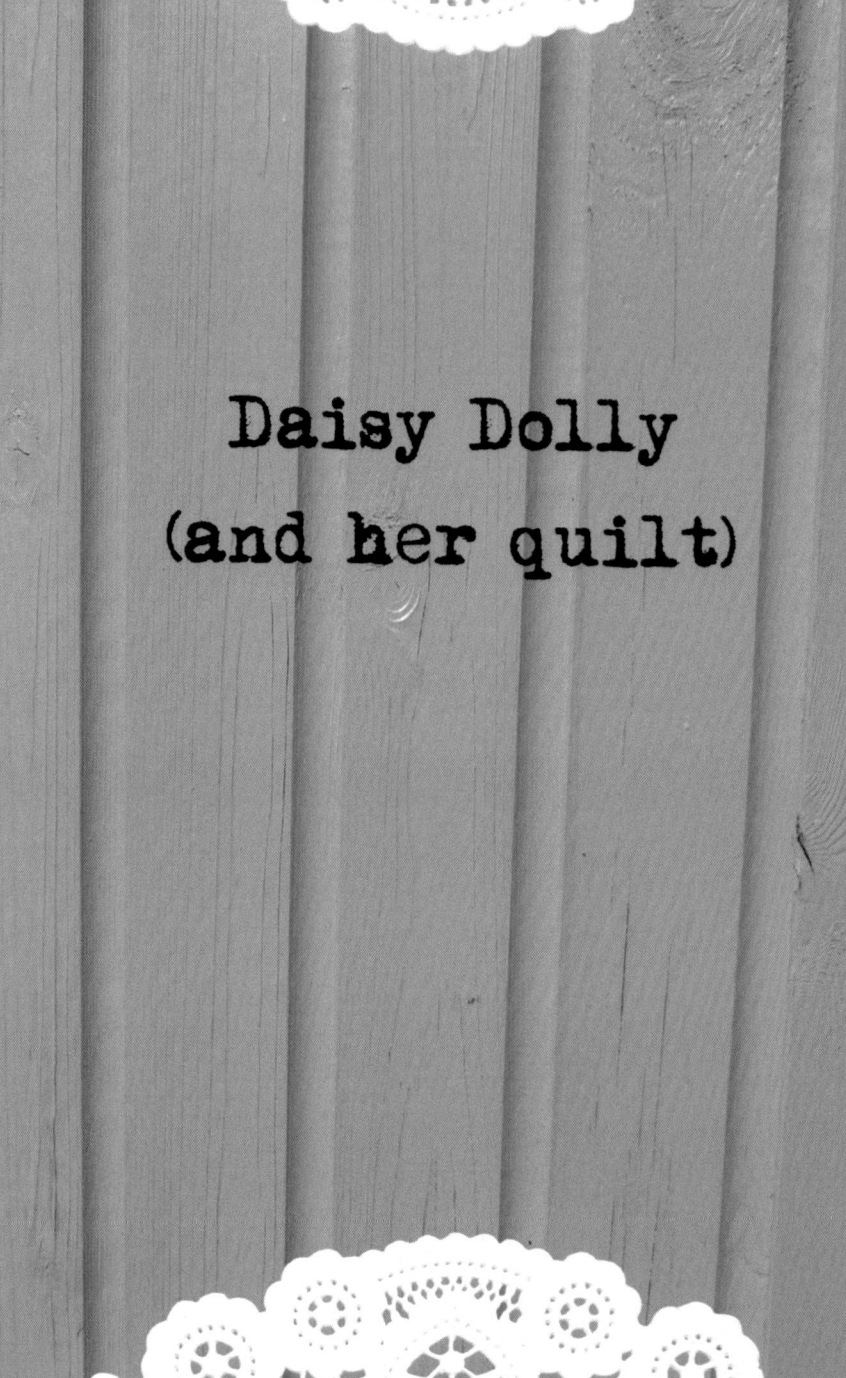

Daisy Dolly
(and her quilt)

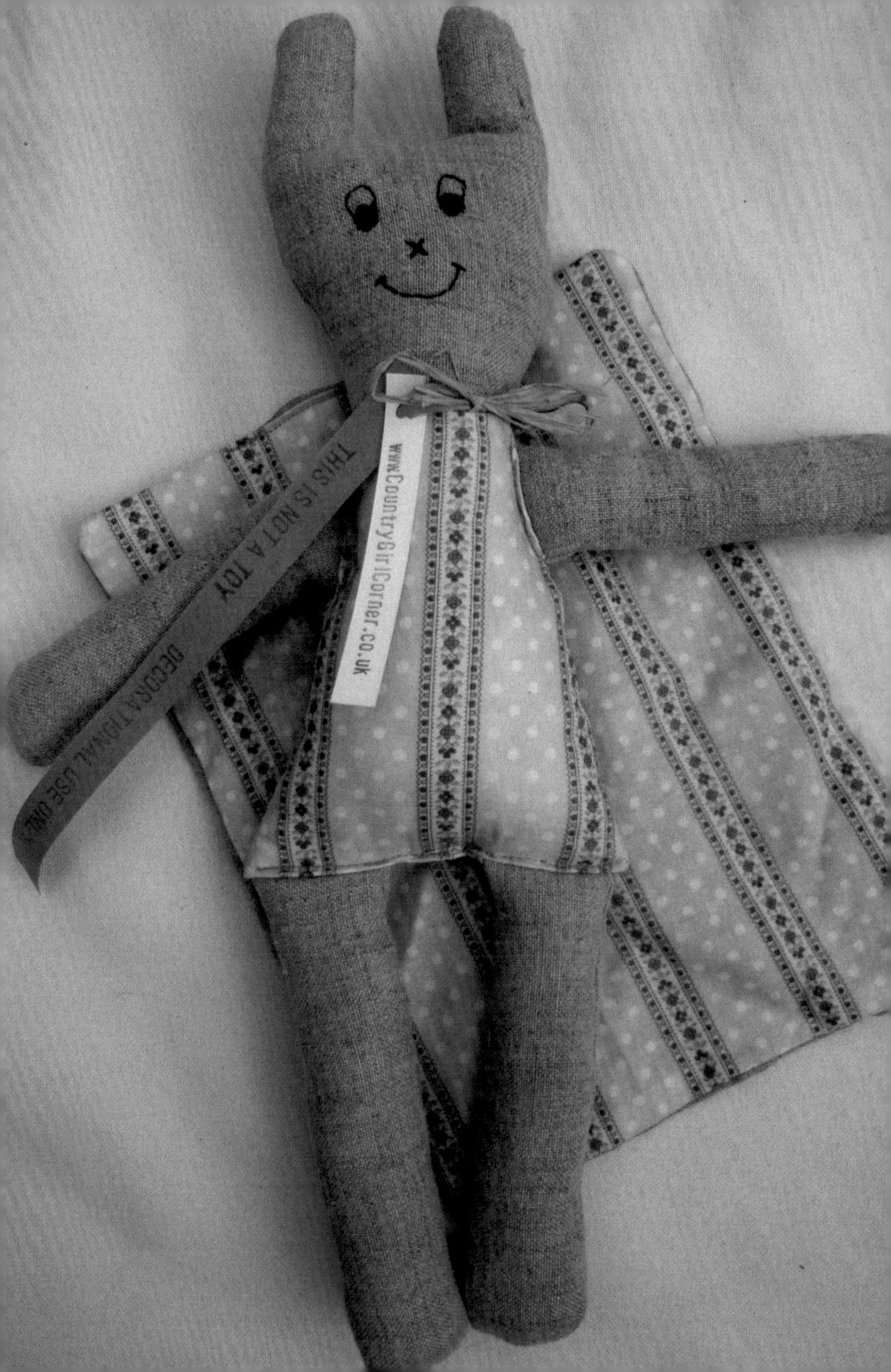
www.CountryGirlCorner.co.uk
THIS IS NOT A TOY

Daisy Dolly & her quilt

You will need

Linen for the doll head, arms, legs and one side of the quilt
Pretty fabric for doll body and reverse of the quilt
wadding for the quilt 20cm x 16cm (8" x 6")
stuffing for the doll

Trace the pattern pieces, and make a new pattern. Fold the linen in half right sides facing and pin on pattern pieces for the arms and legs. Sew around the pattern pieces and then cut out, Cut out the body from pretty fabric, and the head piece from linen then sew the head pieces to the body sections (right sides together), the with right sides together sew the head and body sides together leaving openings for the arms to be inserted. Snip and turn to right side out. Snip and turn the arms and legs and stuff. You can either put the arms in the openings and sew around by hand, or alternatively put the arms in the holes, pin and sew on the the sewing machine. Stuff the head and the body and then turn up the bottom edge and position the legs in place and either sew the legs and bottom edge in place by hand, or pin the legs in place and sew in the sewing machine.

Cut rectangles of wadding, linen & pretty fabric 20 cm x 16 cm (8" x 6"), place the wadding down first, then linen right side up, followed by the pretty fabric (right side down) Make a sandwich with the three layers and then sew around the sides leaving an opening at one end.

Turn through to right side (between the linen and pretty fabric layers which will then put the wadding in the middle

Slip stitch closed

Sew the face on your dolly, give her a name and she's ready to become your best friend

Stick Leg Doll

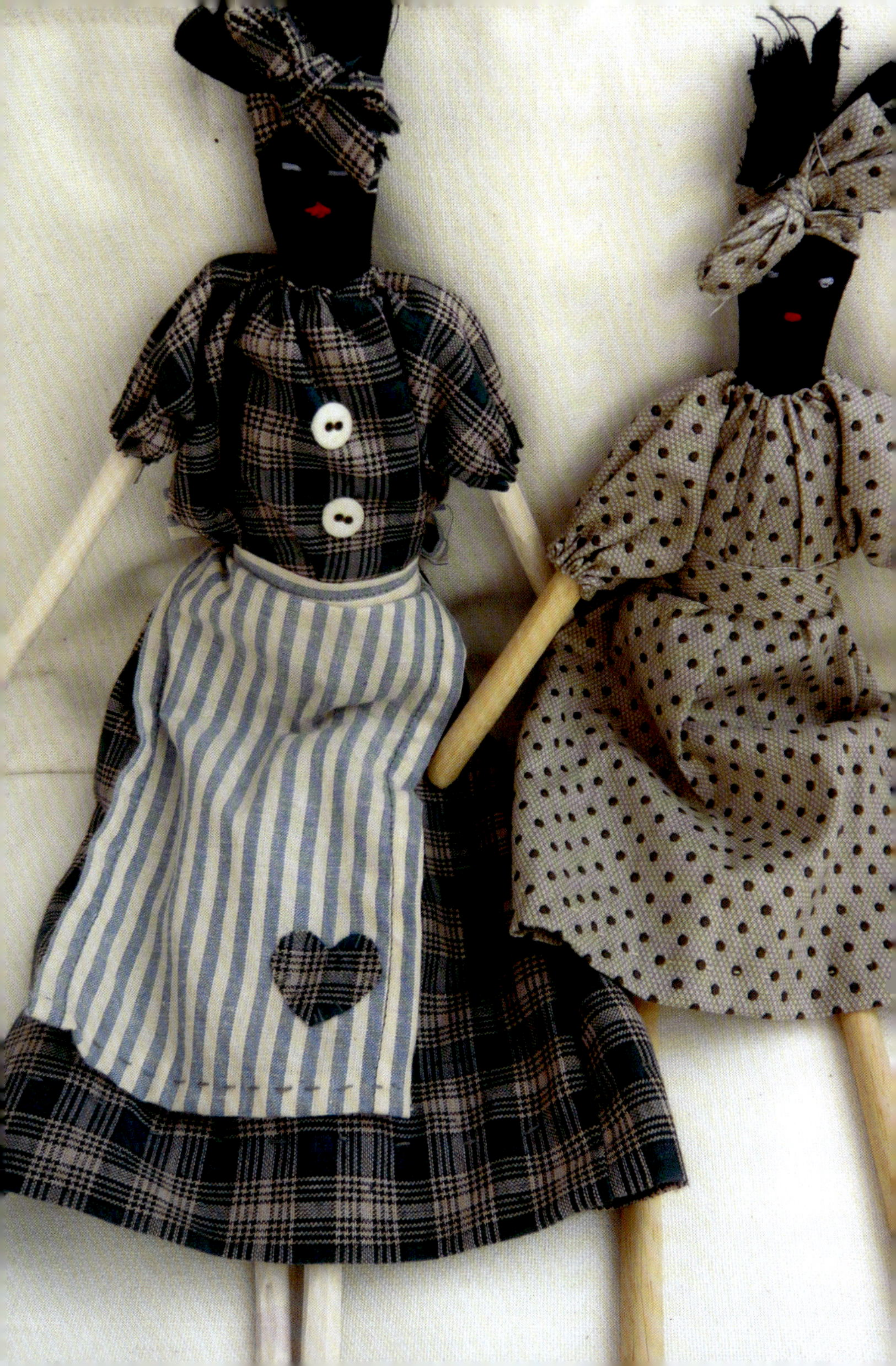

Stick Leg Doll

You will need:

50cm (20") of 7mm (1/4") dia dowel
toy filler
black cotton fabric 20cm x 20cm (8" x 8")
length embroidery thread
white fabric / underwear 18cm x 10cm (7" x 4")
dress fabric/contrasting apron fabric
22cm x 45cm (9" x 18")

Cut the dowel into 2 pieces 15cm (6") long and 2 piece 10cm (4") long Drill a hole in the end of the dowel sticks. Cut out the body pattern piece and pin to a double layer of fabric (right sides together) sew around, cut out and turn to right side. Stuff and sew closed (don't leave an opening)
Take a large needle and embroidery thread and sew the dowel sticks to the body (longer sticks for legs/shorter for arms). Sew through the hole and straight through the body piece and then tie the embroidery thread in a double knot to fasten. You want to leave the stick with some movement so don't tie it on too tightly to the body.
Rip lengths of your remaining black fabric into strips approx 1 1/2cm x 8cm (5-8 pieces) (1/2" x 3") and tie a loose knot in the middle of each piece. Sew these pieces along the top edge of the head (sew the knots to the head) and then trim the ends (the more raggedy the better)

Cut the dress pattern piece and with right sides together sew the sides/arms together leaving the neck and arm holes open.

Place the dress on the doll and then with a double thread, turn in the neck edge and sew a running stitch around and pull to gather the dress around the neck and secure the thread. Do the same for the arms of the dress

Turn up the bottom of the dress and hem.

Optional

Cut out a piece of apron fabric 6cm x 10cm (2 1/2" x 4") and hem each side, sew to a strip of fabric long enough to fit around the doll and tie in a bow at the back.

Fold the underwear fabric in half right sides together and sew down the side. Follow the sewing line on the pattern, sew up, across and down and then cut up between the sewing line to create the two legs.

Turn the underwear to the right side out and place on doll. Turn over the top edge and sew a running stitch around and then pull to gather around the waist of the doll. Turn up the leg edges and hem

Sew eyes in blue / lips in red
(just a few stitches as shown)

You can adapt the pattern to make smaller dolls, and you can add an apron, and a head scarf to make each doll look unique and then give them names and give to someone to love

Hug in a rug

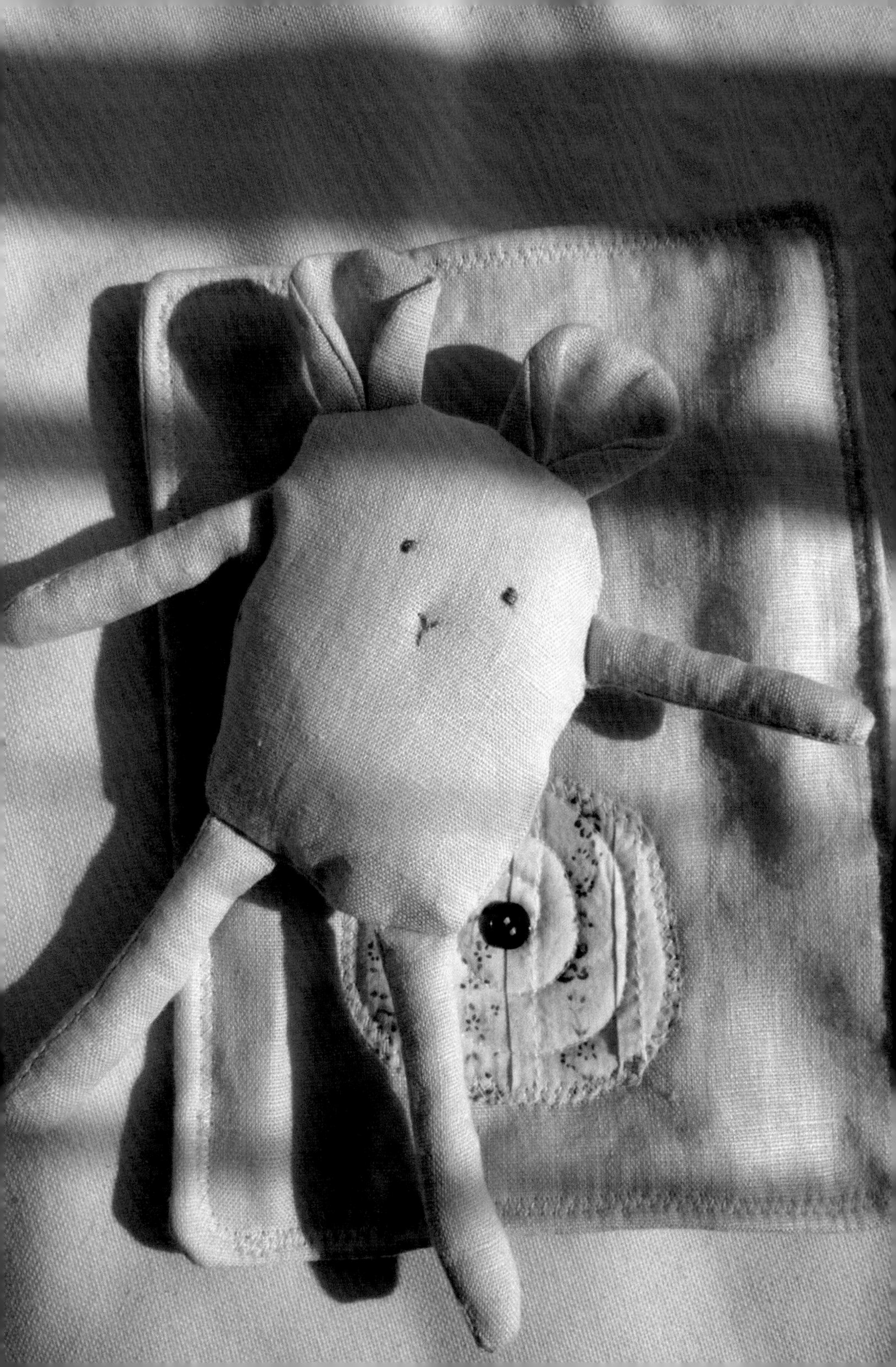

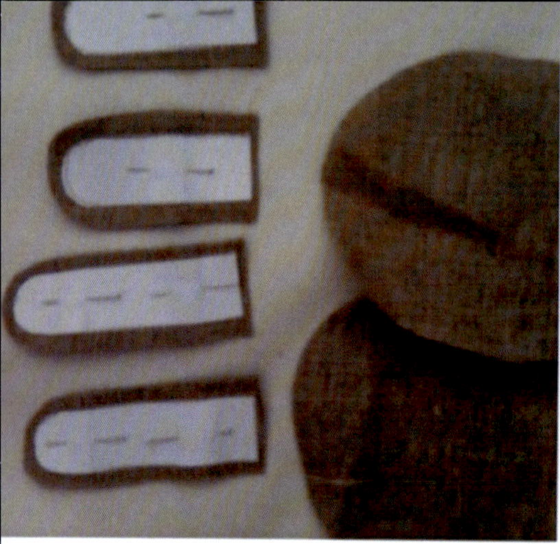

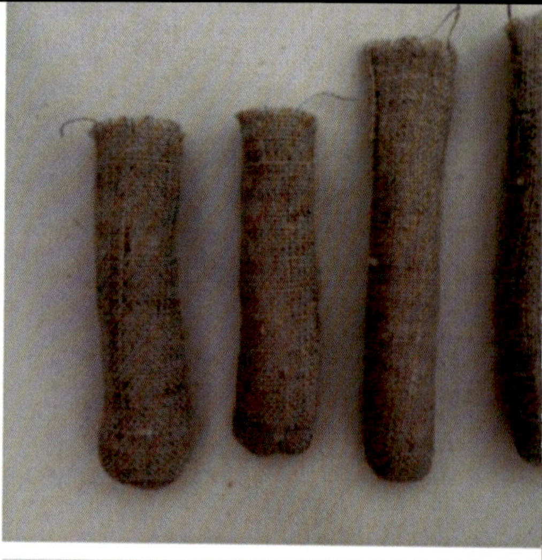

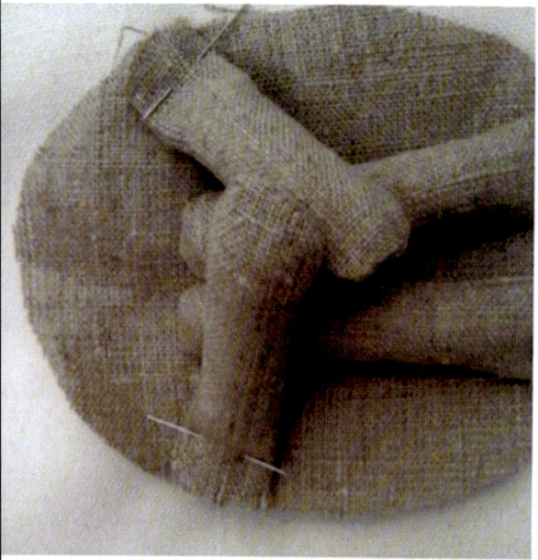

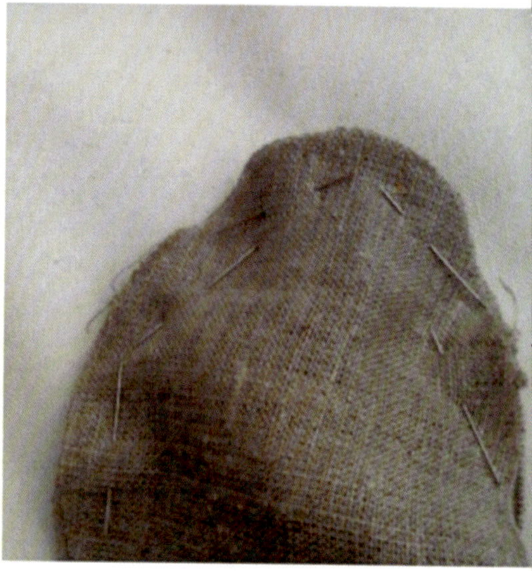

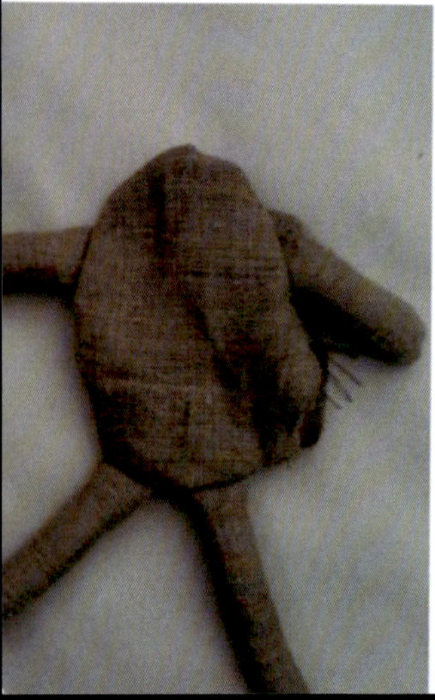

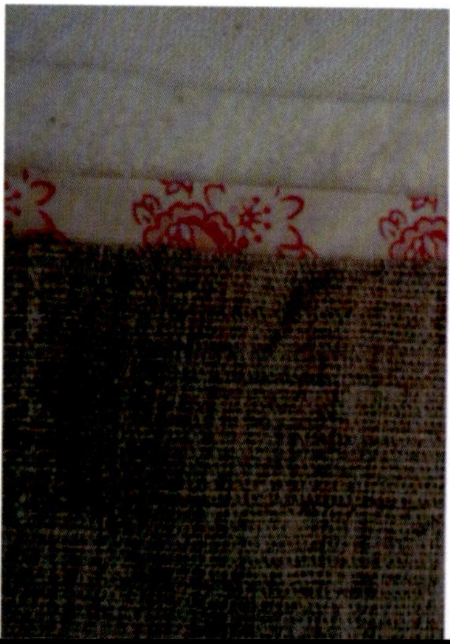

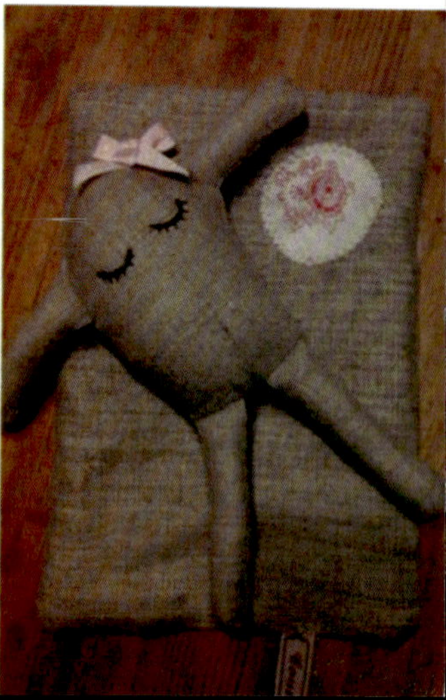

Hug in a Rug

You will need:

Fat quarter plain linen
4cm x 4cm (1 1/2" x 1 1/2") pretty fabric
toy filler
piece wadding 18xcm x 15cm (7" x 6")
1 small button

Cut two pieces of your main fabric 18 x 15cm (7" x 6")
Cut a circle of your pretty contrasting fabric
and position it on one of your pieces of linen
Sew around the circle in a zig zag stitch
to secure in place, sew the button in the centre

Lay the wadding piece down first, followed
on top by the linen (right side up) followed
by the pretty fabric right side down
Sew around the edges leaving a 4cm (1 1/2")
opening at one of the short edges.
Turn to the right side out so you have the
wadding sandwiched in the middle. Tuck in
the raw edge and sew across to close.
Cut around the body pattern pieces. Fold the linen
fabric right sides facing and pin on pattern
pieces for the arms, legs and ears. Sew around
the leg and arm pieces and turn to the right
side out and stuff, sew the ear pieces (right
sides together) and turn to right side out
(the ears are optional, sometimes I don't
put the ears on, but instead sew a bow to
the top of the head) The legs, arms, and ears
all need to be sandwiched between the body pieces,
so pin the legs, arms and ears to one of the body
pieces all facing the centre
Place the remaining body piece on top and sew
around leaving a 3cm (1") gap at one side of the body
Sew around and then turn to right side out,
stuff and sew across the opening
Sew a few stitches for the face

Bear in a box

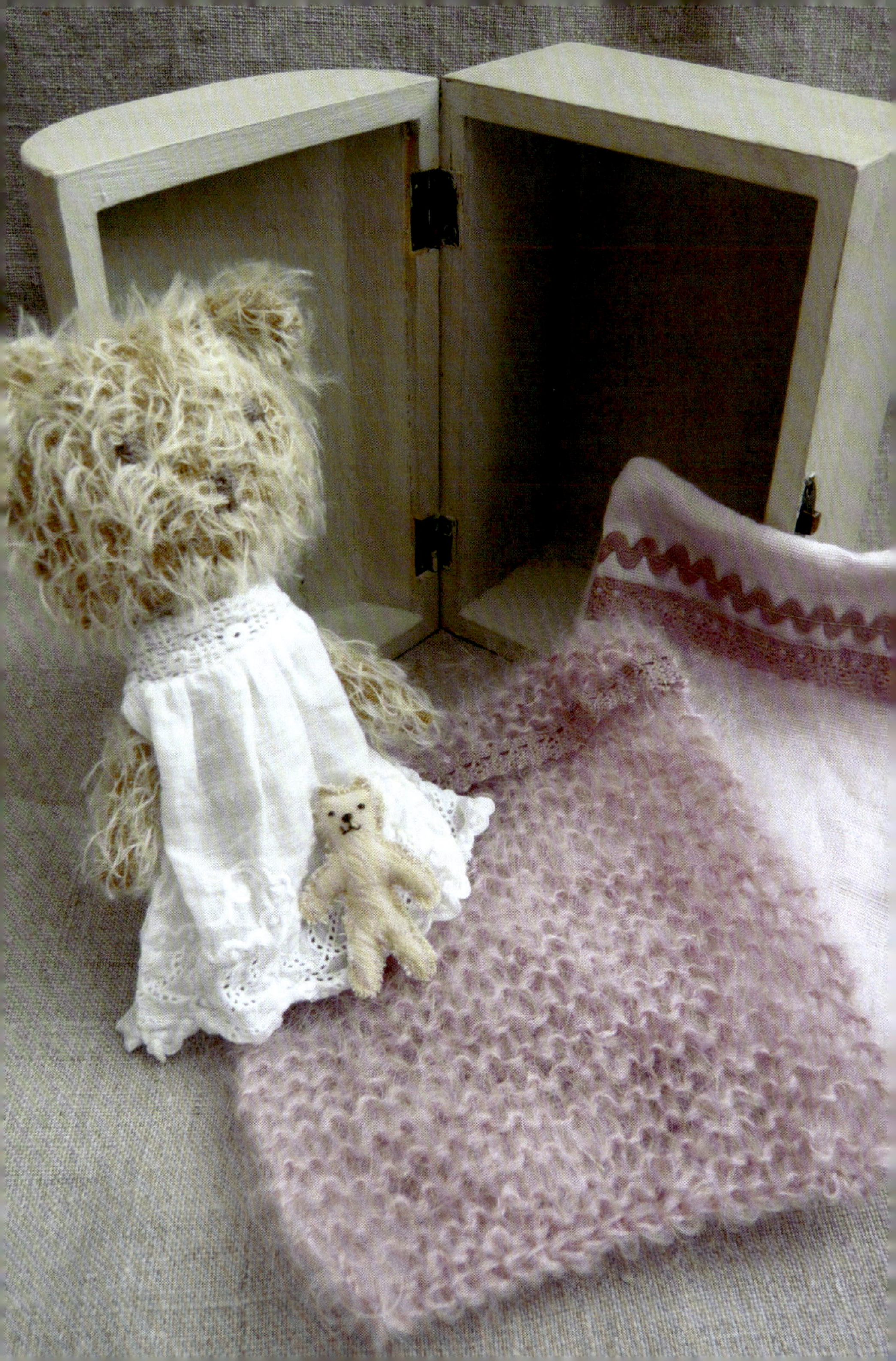

The Bear In A Box

You will need:

mohair fabric 22cm x 22cm (9" x 9")
toy stuffing
dress fabric 2 pieces 10cm x 12cm (4" x 5")
wooden box, paint, sandpaper, wax
mohair dk wool/ribbon trim
scraps of fabric and wadding for quilt
10cm x 12cm (4" x 5")

Trace the pattern pieces and pin on the reverse of the mohair fabric and cut out.
Sew two ear pieces together right sides together and repeat for other ear. Turn to right side out. Pin these to one of the head pieces with the raw edges lined up with the outer edge of the head and sew in place.
Take the other head piece and with right sides together (and the ears sandwiched between) sew around the edge leaving the neck edge open. Turn to right side out and stuff.
Fold the body, arms and legs pieces in half and sew leaving the top ends open, turn through to right side and stuff (turning these pieces is quite difficult, but be patient, try chop sticks/various tools from a manicure kit - or a proper turning tool!) Run a gathering stitch around the bottom of the head neck edge and pull to tighten and secure thread. Turn in the top of the body and sew to the head (the back seam should be down the back) Turn in the open edges of the arms and legs and sew to the body.
I normally sew the nose feature onto the mohair nose piece before I sew it to the head, so use a darker thread colour so the features will show up, and then hem and sew the nose piece to the front of the face, and then sew the eyes in place.

To knit the blanket, cast on approx 10cm (4") (normally 18 stitches) and knit each row until you have approx 12cm (5") of knitting, cast off and sew in the loose ends. sew a little ribbon trim across the top of the blanket.

The quilt is made by putting the wadding and fabric right side up, and the other piece of fabric right side down. Sew around leaving an opening of 5cm (2") at one end. Turn to right sides out and sew across the open end.

The box is painted with an oil based paint and left to dry. Once dry, sandpaper over the whole box paying particular attention to the edges to remove most of the paint. Then take a coloured furniture wax and rub over the box and then wipe off excess to give an aged look. For the small bear, fold the fabric with the right sides out, and pin the pattern on. Cut the fabric out around the edge of the pattern - there is no seam allowance. Starting at the neck edge, and using a top stitch, sew around the head, and then stuff. Then carefully sew down the top edge of one arm and then roll a small sausage shape of filler and hold it in the length of the arm and sew around the end of the arm and up the inside of the arm, continue in this way around the legs and back up the other side of the body, stuffing as you go. Sew on face features with a darker contrasting thread.

Place the two dress pieces together right sides together and sew half way up each side, iron seam open then turn down 1cm (1/4") across the top edges and sew across creating a channel. Turn to right side out and thread the ribbon through the channel, place on bear and pull to gather. Hem bottom edge / add trim to decorate.

Raggedy Anne

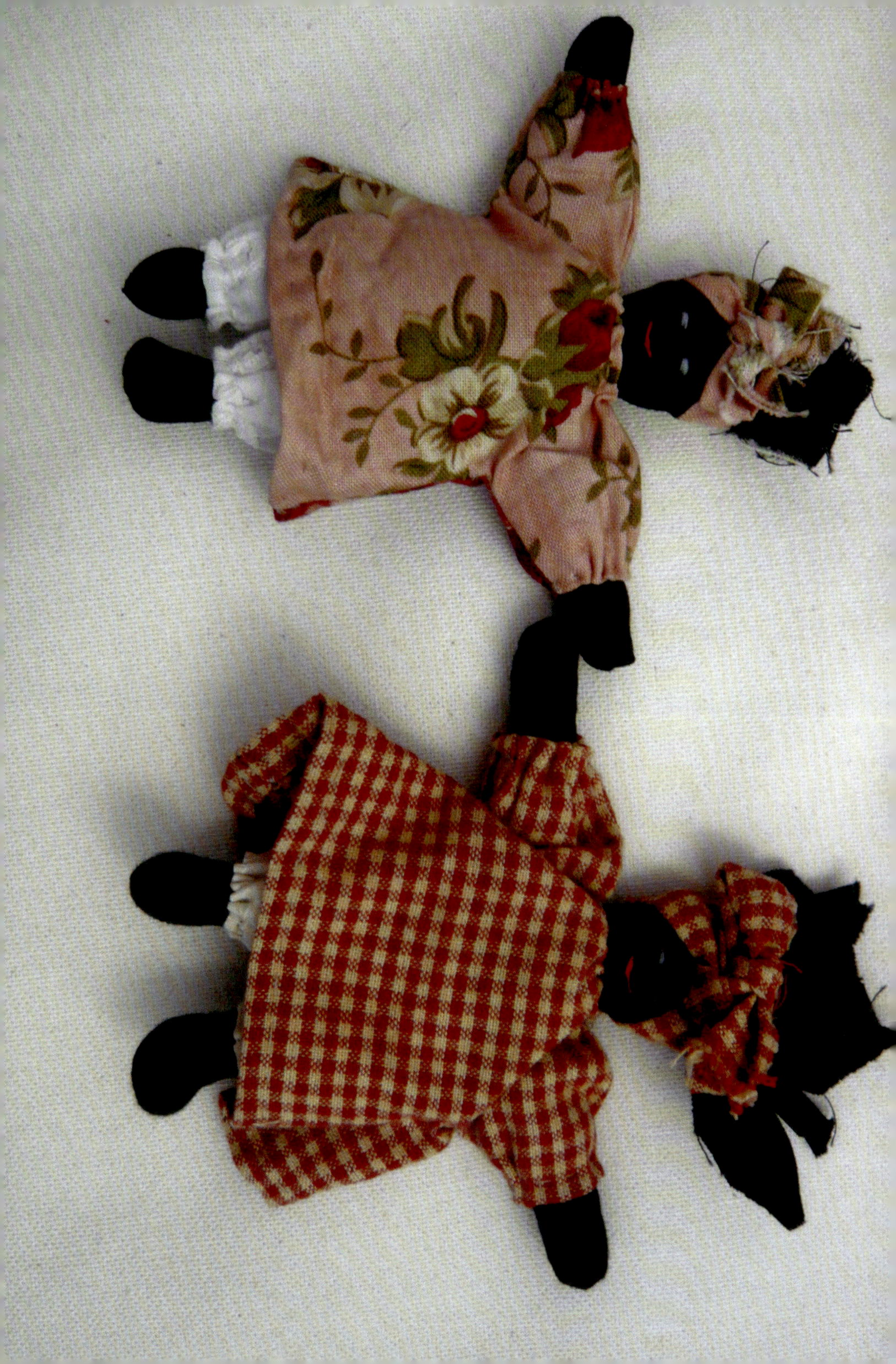

Raggedy Anne

You will need:

Piece black cotton 12cm x 28cm (4 1/2" x 11")
toy filler
piece dress fabric 14cm x 16cm (5 1/2" x 6")
hair band 3cm x 28cm (1" x 11")
underwear fabric 10cm x 15cm (4" x 6")

Trace the pattern pieces and make new pattern pieces. Fold body fabric right sides facing and pin on pattern pieces (the pattern is the sewing line) Sew around the pattern pieces leaving openings as indicated, cut around pieces Turn each piece to right side out and stuff with filler. Fold in bottom of body and insert tops of legs and sew across. Turn in the open edge of the arms and sew the arms to the side of the body. Cut 6 strips from remaining body fabric, 1/2cm x 4cm (1/4" x 1") and tie a knot in the middle of each strip. Sew the middle of the knots to the top of the head seam. Wrap the hair tie around the head and tie at front, sew a few stitches around the top and bottom of band to keep in place

For the underwear, fold the fabric in half and sew along side. Sew up, across and down the middle of the underwear as shown, Cut between stitching, snip into curves and turn to right side out. Position on doll. Turn the top edge over and sew a gathering stitch around and pull thread to gather so it fits the doll. Turn under bottom of each leg and sew a gathering thread around, pull up and secure

Cut dress fabric from pattern

Cut head hole and with right sides facing
sew along under arms and down sides
Turn to right side and position on doll
Turn under and hem bottom edge of dress

Turn under sleeve edges, sew gathering
thread around, pull up and secure
Turn under neck edge, sew through and gather

Sew the eyes in blue and the mouth in red
Finish the thread ends by pushing the needle
through to the back of the head and finish
under the edge of the head band

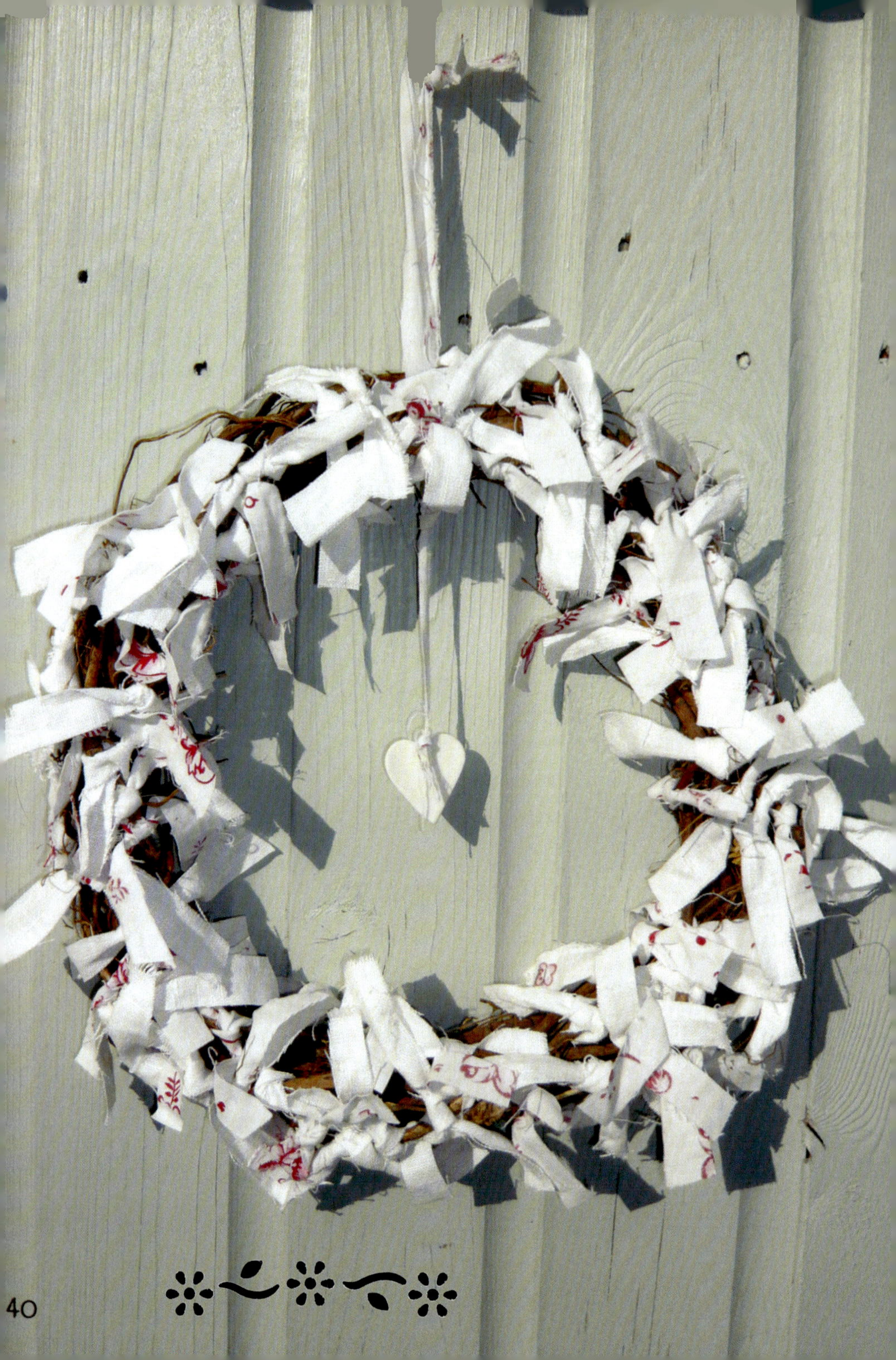

Rag Wreaths

You will need:

A vine wreath 30cm (12") makes a good size
but you can make bigger or smaller depending
on the intended location
Scraps of fabric - you can make any colour
(natural linen with a little splash of red
is nice for Christmas/white linen is a good
shabby chic look)
A crochet hook/chopstick/pencil (a good
poke stick)
25cm (10") ribbon (or contrasting fabric strip)
to make a loop to hang
optional: small robin bird with wires
attached to feet

Vine wreaths tend to be a little more flexible
than willow wreaths and make it easier to work
with, but any type of wreath will do because
you are only using it as a base to hold the fabric,
You can completely fill the wreath
with fabric knots, or you can space the fabric
knots so you can see the wood between
- depends on your personal preference - try a
section and see (you can always add
more knots)

Cut (or rip) strips of fabric 12cm x 2cm (5" x 1/2")
approx (if you rip the fabric along with grain
the fraying adds a little extra texture
Push one half of each strip under one of the
strands of vine and tie a knot

Work around the wreath placing the knots evenly (you only need to do the front if the wreath is going to be hung on a wall/door)
Continue until you have completed the circle. Add more knots until you are happy with the result
Turn the wreath to the back, and tie a ribbon for hanging at the top securing it carefully around a number of the vine strands

At Christmas you can secure a little robin at the bottom of the wreath

At Easter you can get little mini eggs with wires attached (from a florist supplier) and fix these around the wreath

You can make a white linen version, then add a little heart hanging in the middle which looks attractive

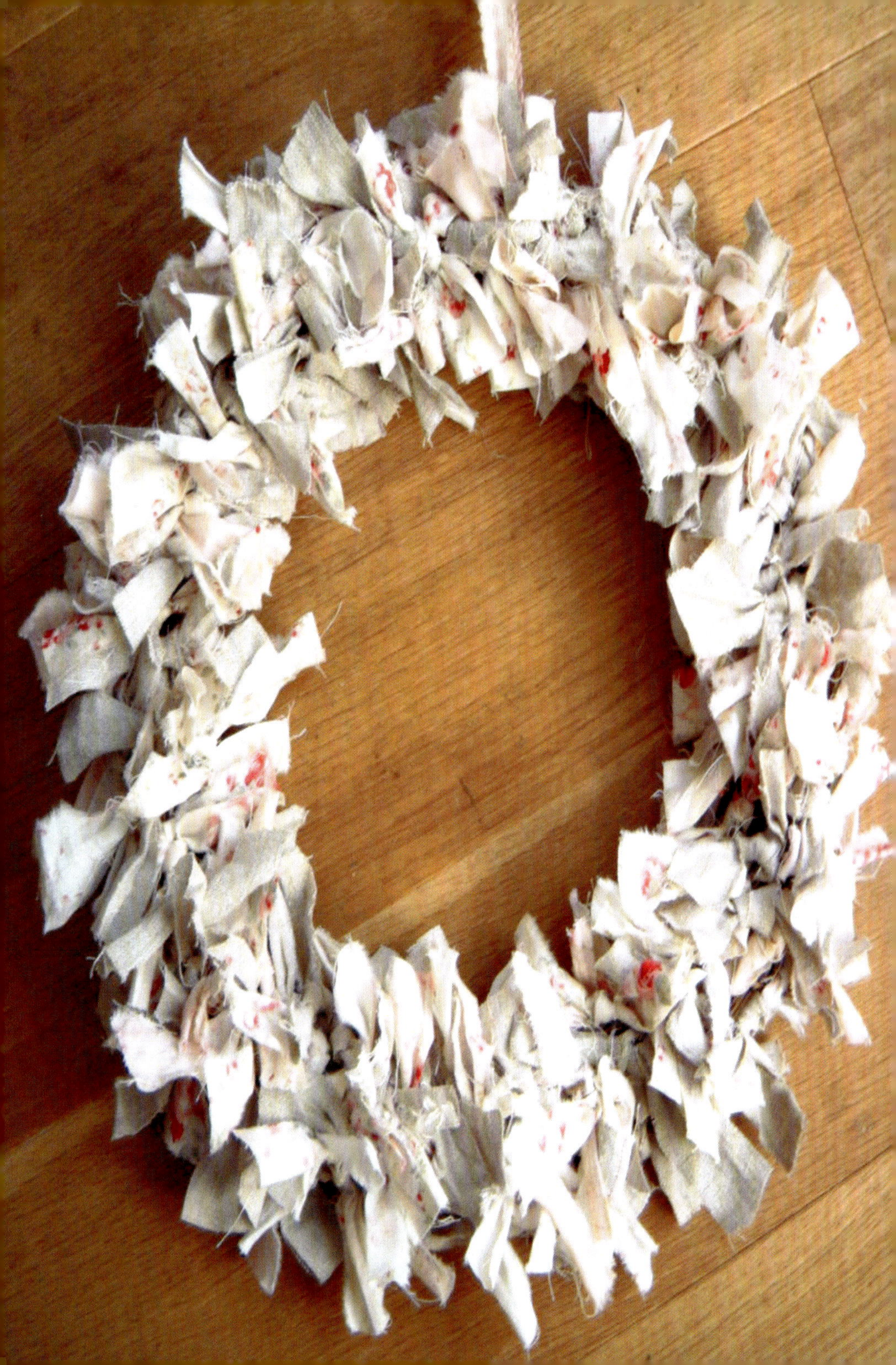

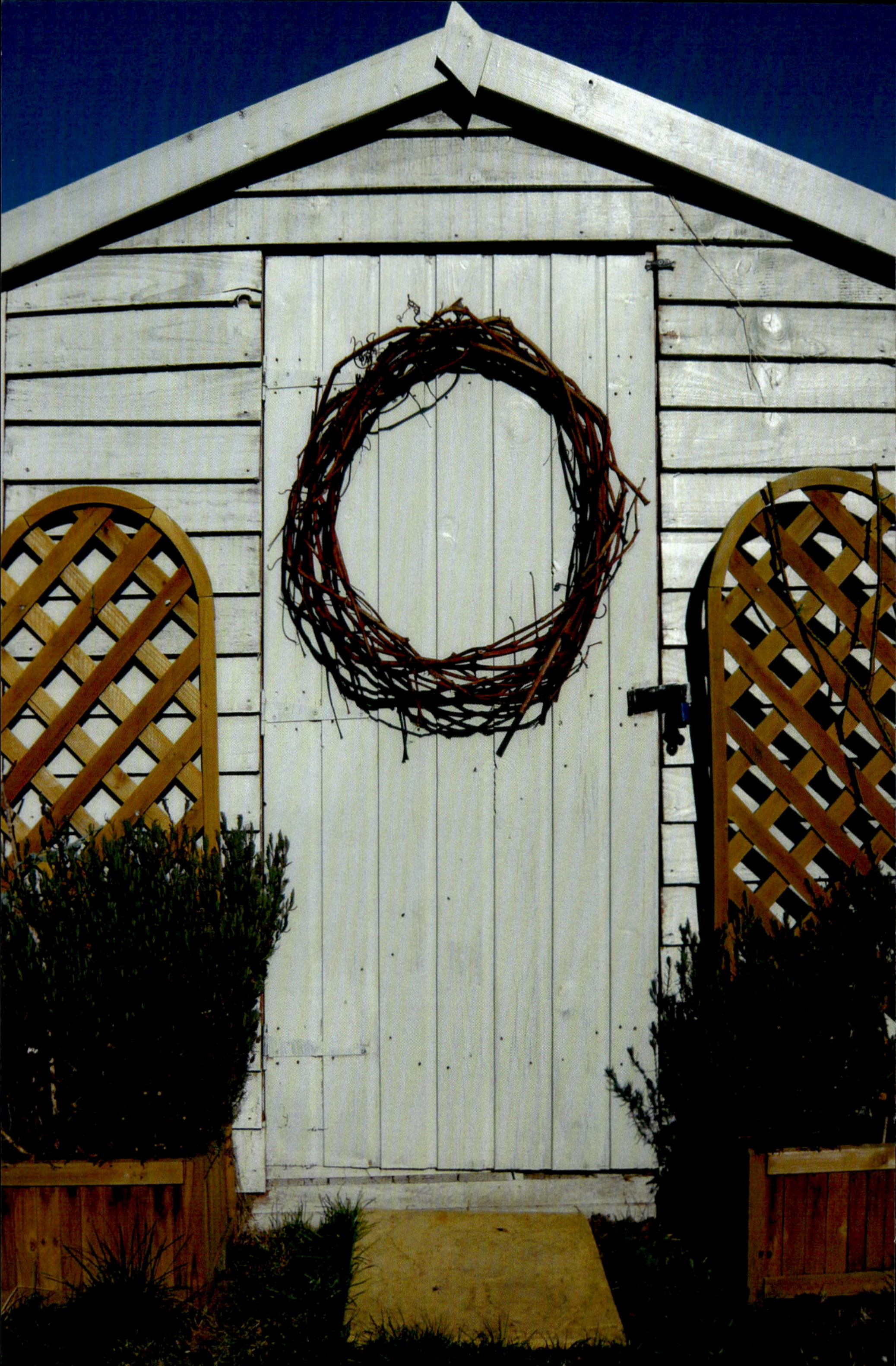

Lavender Hearts..................

Fold Fabric right sides together, pin on pattern and sew around. Leave a gap along one side and also a small gap in the top centre of the heart. Snip the curves towards the sewing line. Hem and sew a thin strip of fabric long enough to make a loop for your heart. Turn your heart to the right side out, Push the two ends of your long strip into the gap at the top of the heart and sew in place, stuff the heart with toy filler and lavender and sew the open edge closed

Bird Mobile

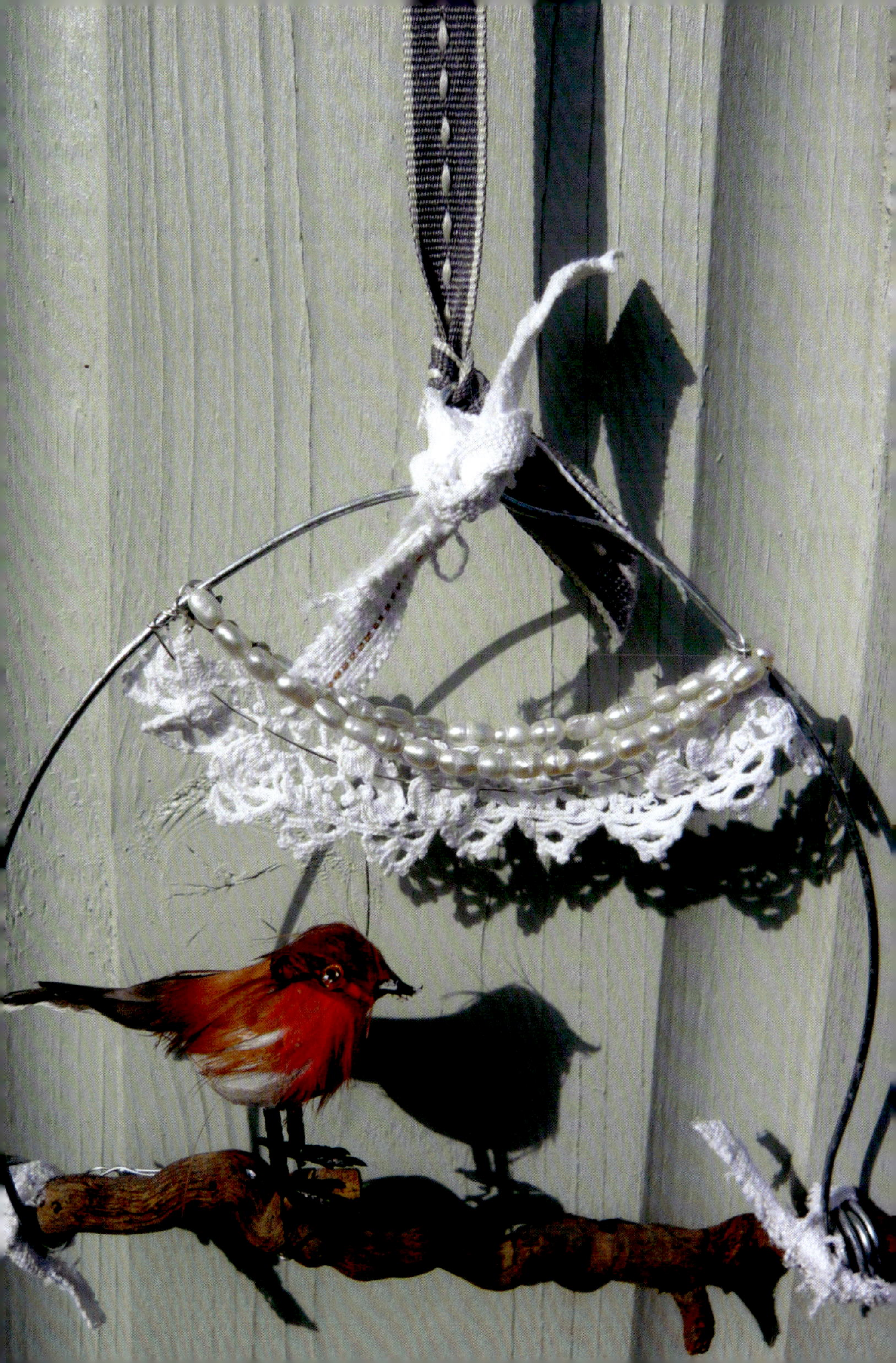

Bird Mobile

You will need

An attractive stick approx 20 cm (8") long, (the thickness of a pencil), you are looking for something with character, a nice curve, a little wriggle in the middle, or possibly some drift wood.
50cm (20") galvanised wire (DIY shop - it won't rust)
thin silver wire - for clothes line
scraps of vintage fabric
small bird with wire on the feet (from florist suppliers or Ebay)
length of ric-rac or ribbon to tie

With plyers twist the wire around the stick at one side, don't forget to make the loop in the top, and take it back down and twist around at the other side of the stick, ensure you don't leave any rough edges. (this should be the approximate size of a side plate)
Twist the thinner wire from one side of the frame to the other, leaving a gentle curve ready to decorate.
Attach your bird by tightly winding the wire below the birds feet around the stick. (you can give the wire a blob of glue to ensure he doesn't fall off)
Cut small rectangles of fabric, fold in half over the thin 'clothes line' and stitch in place you can tie on little bits of ribbon, or torn fabric to decorate.
At Christmas you can cut out small 'stocking' shapes and sew those onto the 'clothes line' or you can thread lengths of lace across the 'clothes line' for a shabby chic look.
Tie your ric-rac to the loop at the top, and hang from the centre of a curtain pole in front of a window............

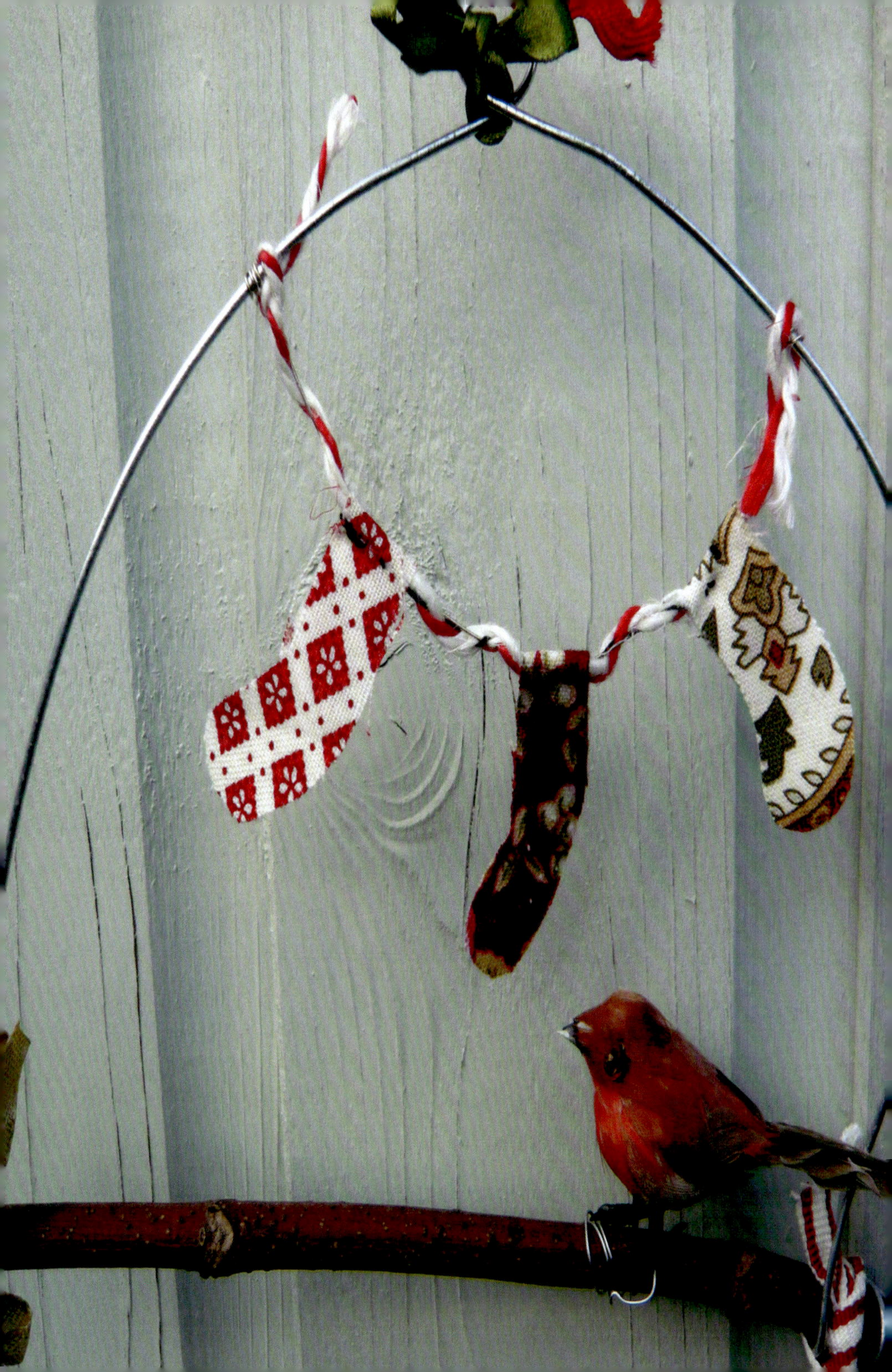

Flowerpot lavender bag

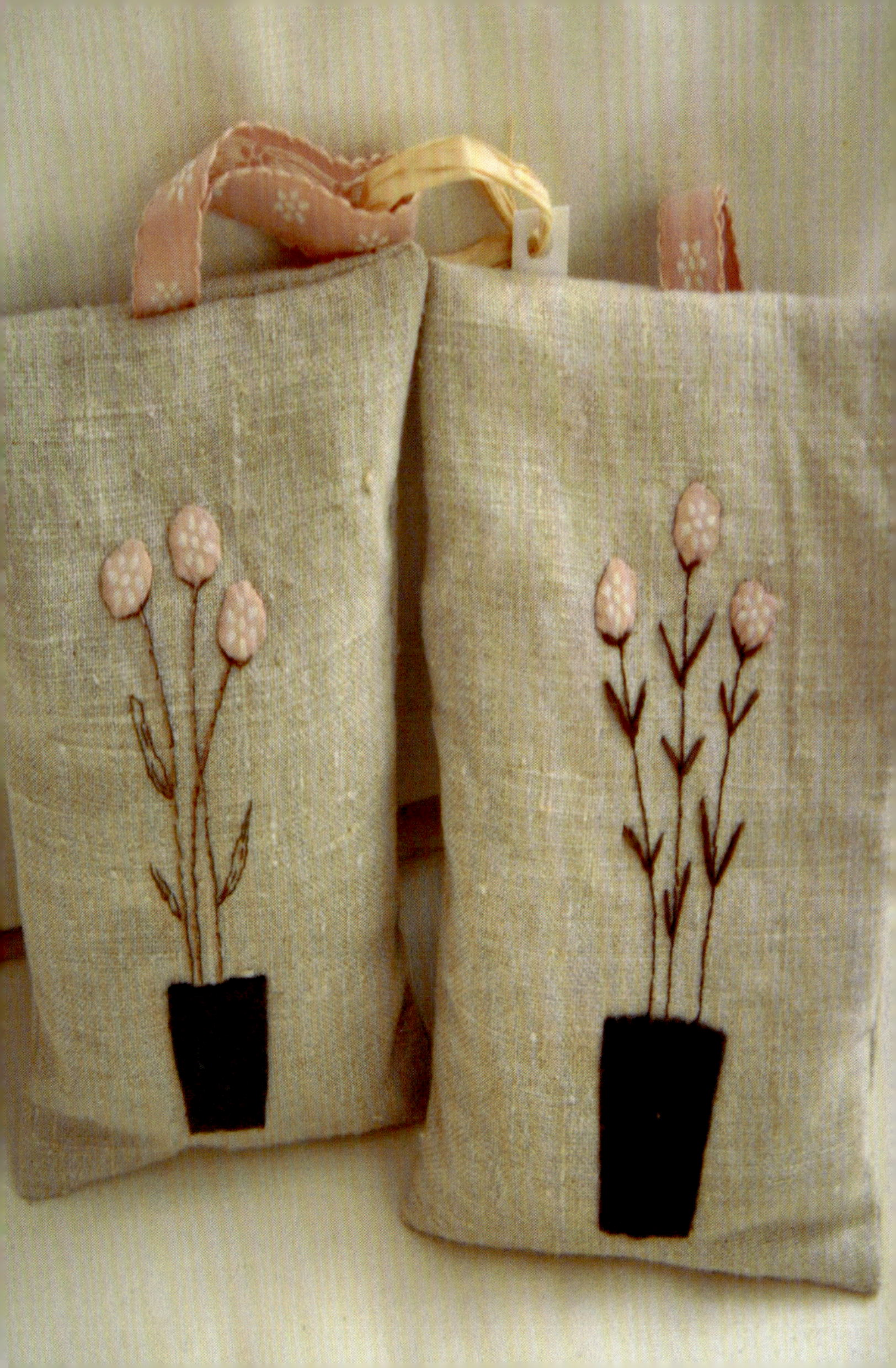

Flowerpot lavender bags

You will need:

2 x pieces linen 16cm x 14cm (6" x 5")
1 piece ribbon 20cm (8")
handful toy filler
handful dried lavender
small piece fabric with small flowers
small piece brown fabric 4cm x 4cm (1 1/2" x 1 1/2")
brown embroidery thread

Fold the small piece of brown fabric into a flowerpot shape (wider at the top than the bottom) and press the seams with your fingers to make a crease. Pin this to one piece of linen, centered and approx 4cm (1 1/2") from the bottom edge. Hand sew this using small stitches and secure the thread at the back. Next cut 4 small pieces from your floral fabric, these should be approx the size of a finger nail. Using the picture as a guide, position each piece approx 6-8 cm (3-4") above your 'flowerpot', arrange and pin in place. Take the pin out from one of the pieces, and keep it in position with your thumb. Next take your needle, and with the edge of the needle carefully turn under the edge of the fabric and hold in place, bring your threaded needle up from the back and through the turned over edge in the small flower, your needle will now be at the front of the fabric so with the side of the needle, turn under the next little bit of edge and then push your needle down through the seam back through to the reverse of the fabric. Keep turning your work until the small flower is stitched in place, secure at the back. Continue this process until all your flowers are on.

Then take your brown embroidery thread through from the back at the top edge of the flowerpot and sew a back stitch line to create the stem, the leaves are just two or three stitches off the main steam, a few on one side and a few on the other, continue up to meet the flowers at the top (you can draw a light pencil mark as a guide) until all the flowers are joined to a stem

Take your piece of ribbon and fold in half (right sides out) and pin to the centre of the top edge of your embroidered piece. Place your other piece of linen on top and pin around the edges.

leave a 6cm (2") opening along the bottom edge and sew around the other sides and turn through to the right side out. Fill with toy filler and lavender (the toy filler helps keep a nice plump shape) and then turn in the open edges, and slip stitch across to close
(you can always open this up again to replenish the lavender)

Hang the bag on the bed post for a good relaxing night sleep

Alternative: Make some lovely romantic lavender bags using white linen, and a vintage fabric heart sewn to the front using a zigzag stitch on the sewing machine
You can add hops and lavender to make 'sleep bags' (see pic page 16)

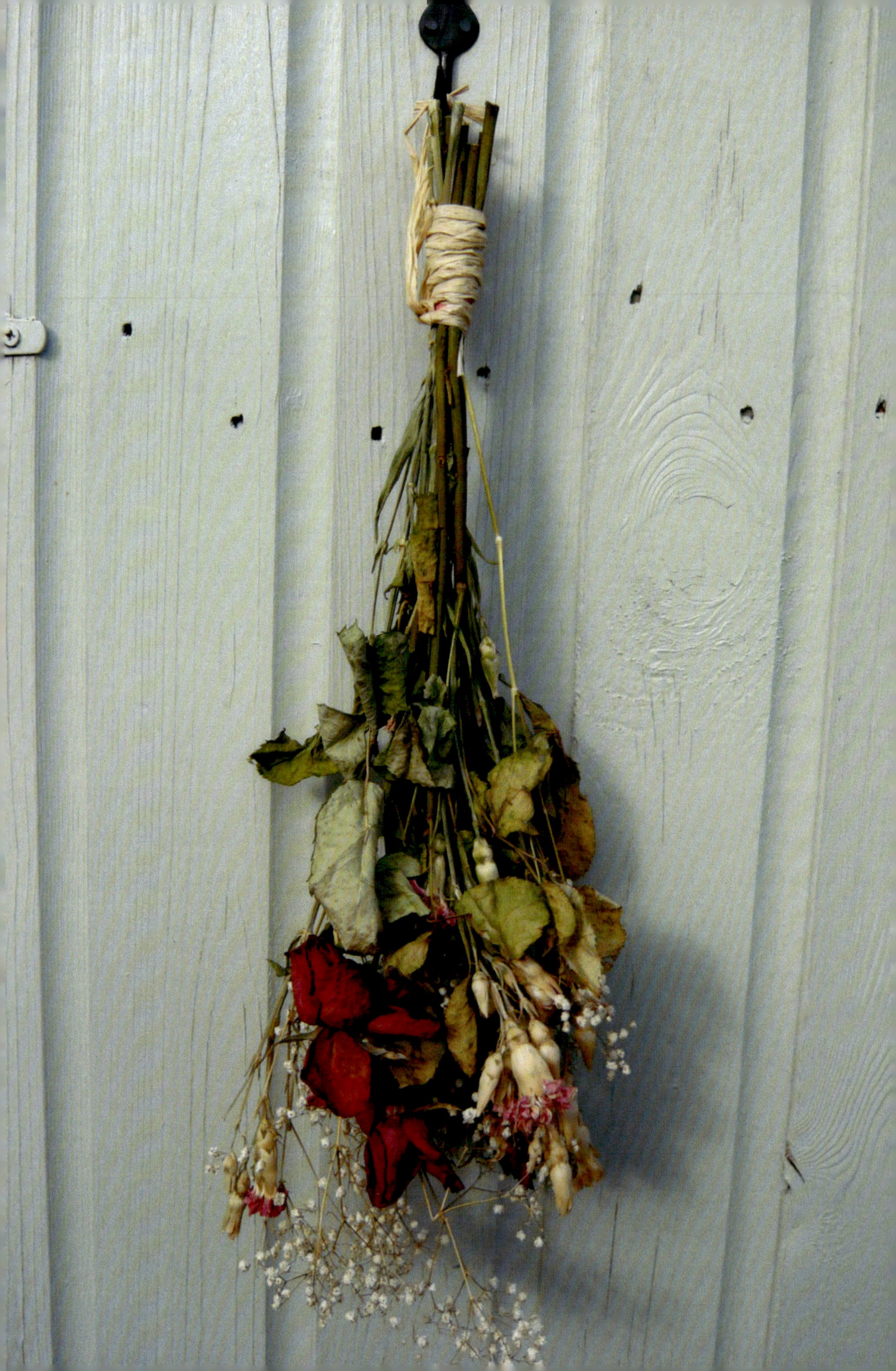

A Mug hug should only be a strip around the middle of the mug, it should not reach from the top of the mug to the bottom otherwise you get a mouthful of wool!!

Cupcake pin cushion

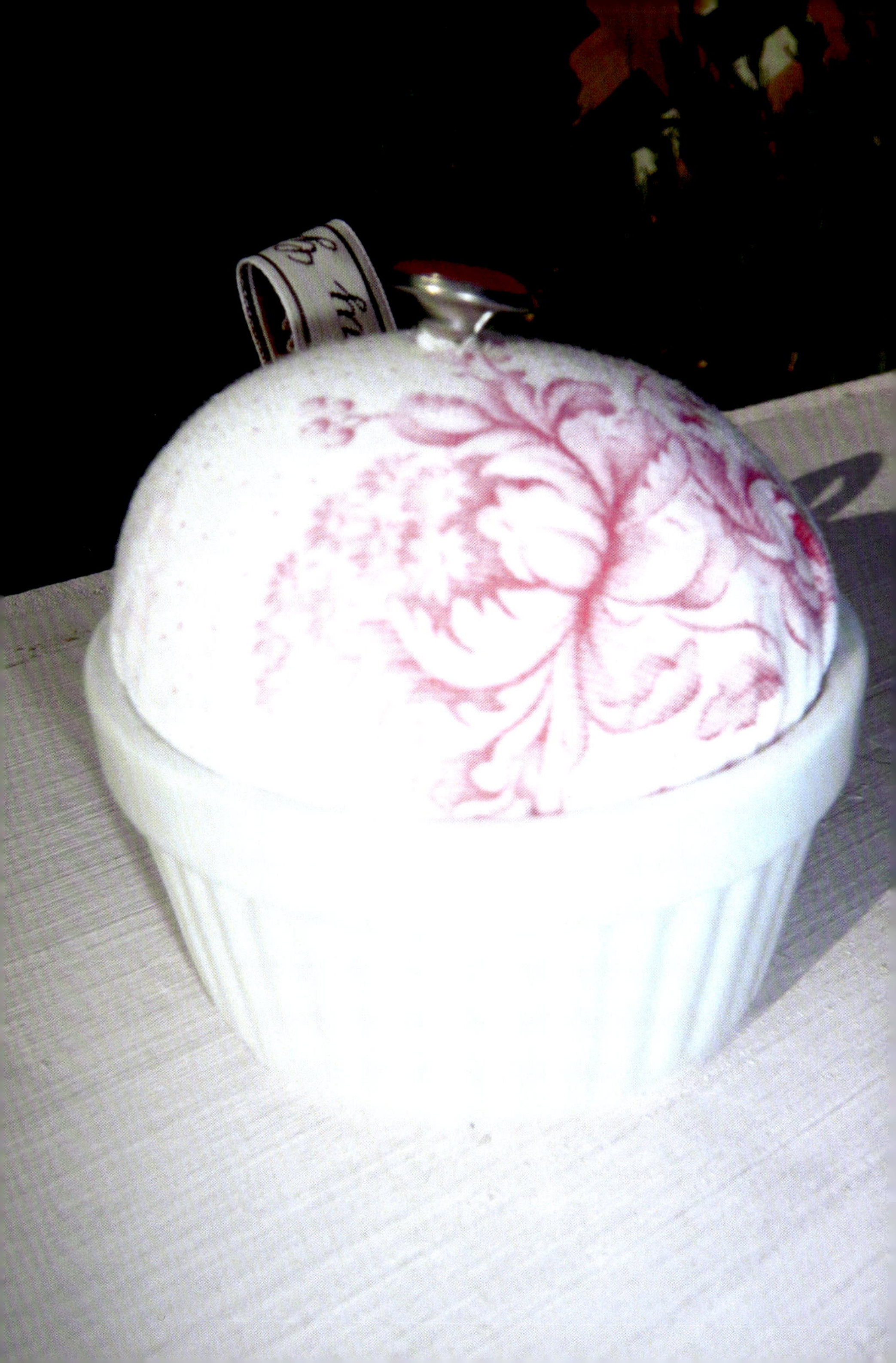

Cup Cake Pin Cushion

You will need:

A ramekin (a white one with ridged sides are best)
piece of felt or wadding for base
piece of fabric for top
large handful of toy filler
a button (I use either a button which looks
like a cherry / or a pearl depending on
my colour scheme)
clear drying glue

Set the ramekin on a piece of paper and draw around the base - this will be the pattern for your felt piece to be glued to the bottom

Next, turn the ramekin upside down and draw around the top edge onto a piece of paper. you will need to draw a circle 4cm (1 1/2") larger than the top of the ramekin, this will then be the pattern for your top fabric.
Cut out your pattern and pin to the top fabric and cut out. Take a length of thread and sew a running stitch around the outside edge approx 1cm (1/4") from the edge, then put a handful of toy filler in the centre and gently pull the thread so it encloses the toy filler in the centre and keep putting filler in until you have a tennis ball size, then pull the thread tight and secure. Check it fits nicely in the ramekin and then glue the inside of the ramekin and squash the ball shape back in position. Sew the button to the top, and glue the felt to the bottom and once dry trim the edge of the felt to neaten

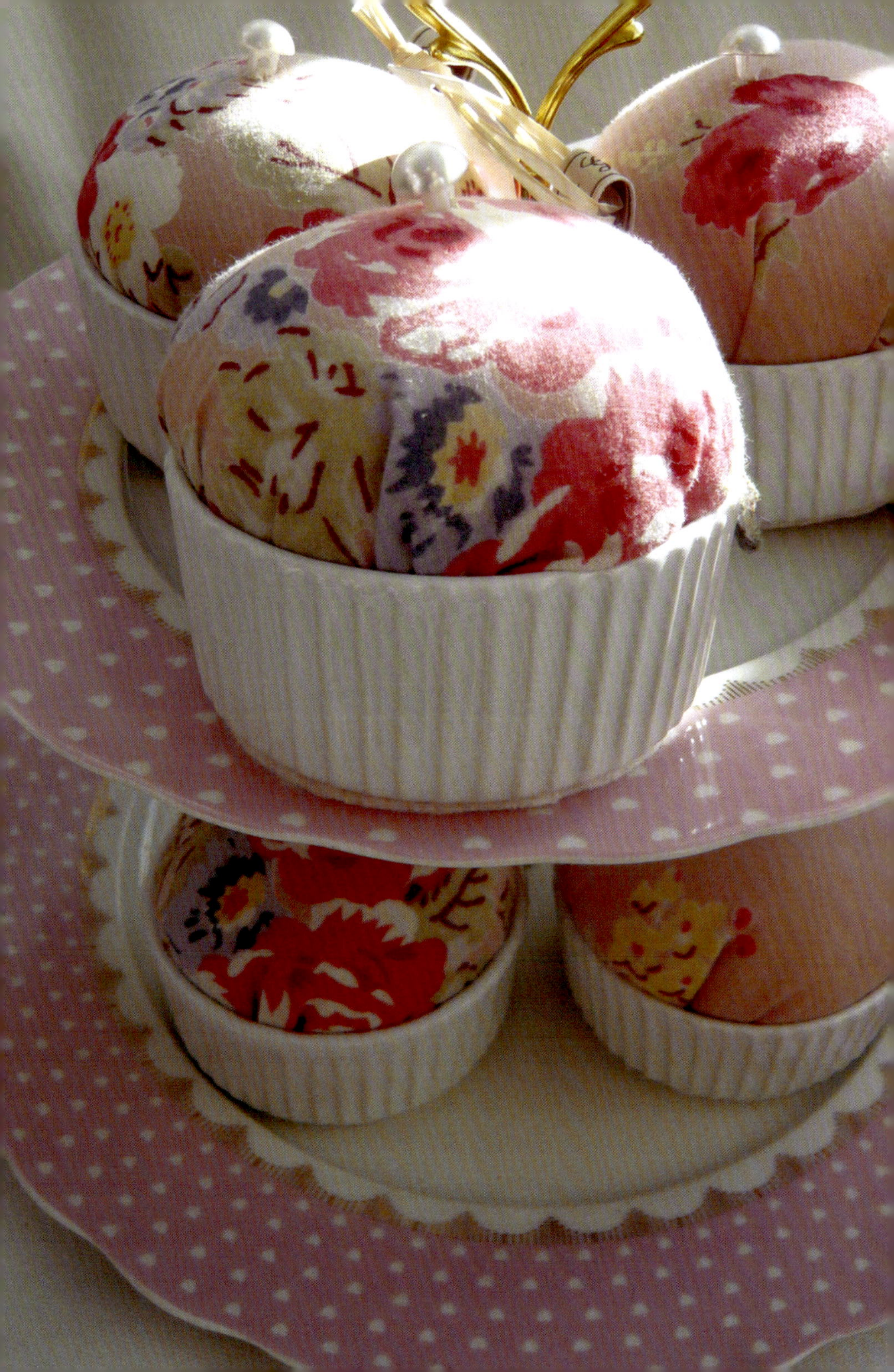

Lavender and wheat bag

Country Girl Corner

www.CountryGirlCor...

Lavender & Wheat Bag

You will need

2 pieces of fabric 45cm x 14cm (18" x 5 1/2")
2 pieces of medium calico 38cm x 14cm (15" x 5 1/2")
500g wheat
handful of dried lavender

From one piece, cut off 6cm (2") and discard then starting on the longer piece, turn in a hem at one end (fold over 1cm (1/4") and fold over again and sew across). Again, take the longest piece and fold over the hemmed edge 5cm (2") from the top (right sides together). Hem the shorter piece and place this on top of the first piece (right sides facing), pin around the edges leaving the top edge open. Starting at the top right edge, sew down the side length, along the bottom (*) and back up the other side. Turn to the right side out, pulling the flap at the top over into position. Make sure all your corners have been pushed out properly. Put back in the machine and sew a line 1cm (1/4") from the edge down the side, along the bottom (*) and back up the other side. This makes the outer of your bag. Cut two calico pieces 38cm x 14cm (15" x 5 1/2") and leaving the top open, sew around the calico piece then turn to the right side out. Fill with wheat and a handful of lavender then turn in the raw edges at the top and sew across. Insert the inner lining bag into the outer and fold the flap over at the top to close

Instructions for use: Microwave for 2 minutes (do not overheat - allow to cool down before re-heating), alternatively put in a plastic bag and put in the freezer and use as cool bag

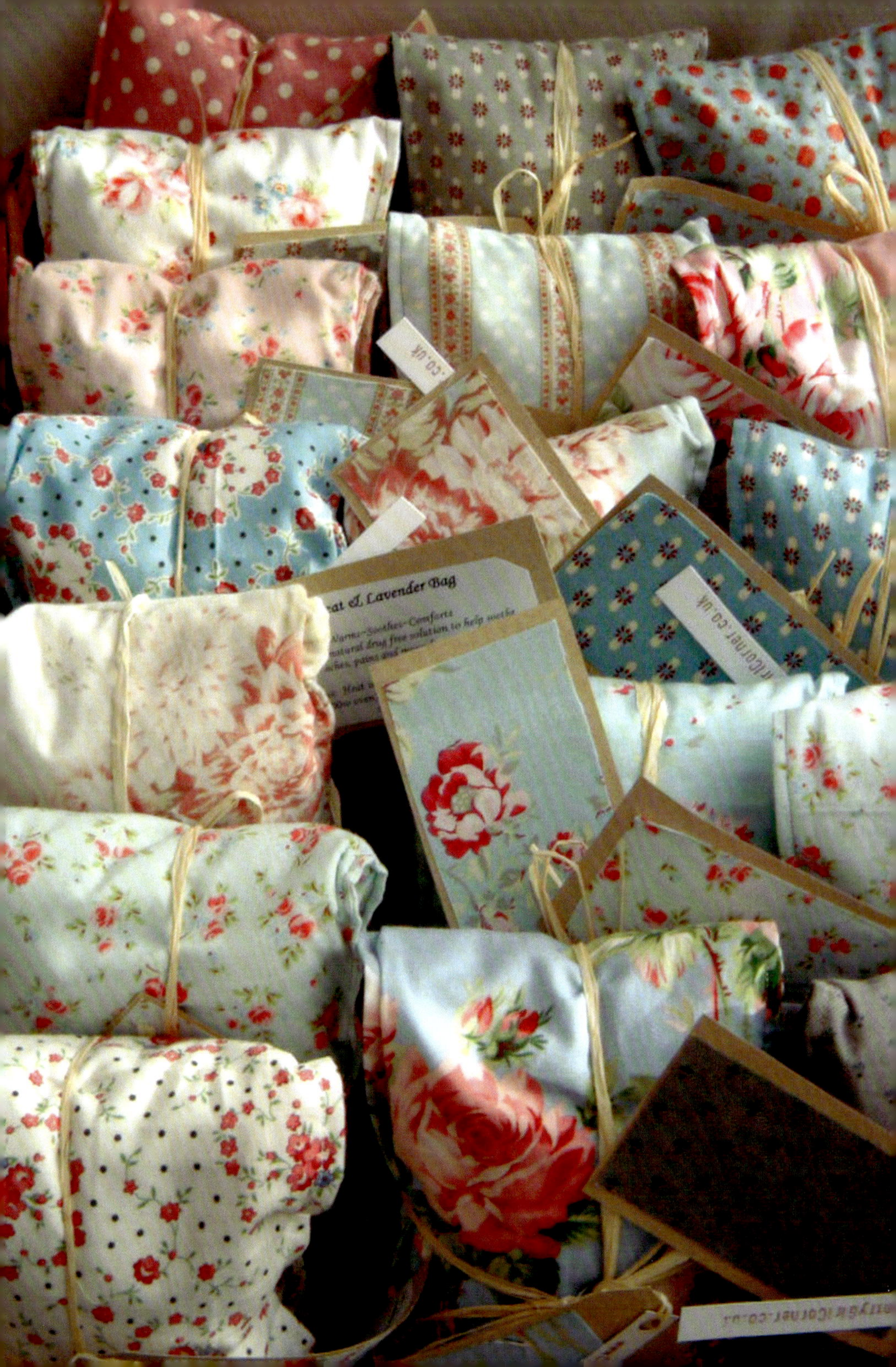
Lavender Bag

The draught excluder
works in the same way
as the cover for the
lavender and
wheat bag only it has
a strap at the end so
you can hang it up on
a coat hook when not
in use.

You will need:
2 pieces 20cm x 90cm (8" x 35")
4 strips pretty fabric
calico / toy stuffing

sew three strips together
and sew to one side
of the linen (alternatively
sew some hearts on)

Make a strap with a length
of linen and pretty
fabric 8cm x 25cm (3" x 10")
(use the instructions for
the straps for the denim bag
page 100)

Follow the directions
for the wheat bag, leaving
the bottom edge open 5cm (2")
where you see the (*) Fold
the strap in half and
slip into the gap at the
bottom edge and
sew across a couple of
times to secure.

Finish the piece the same as
the Lavender & Wheat bag

Big Jam Jars full of little scraps

Three Things........

My normal way of working is to make three of a new design. I'll make one just to get the idea going. I'll make another one to improve on the first one, either in design/speed/ease etc and the third one will be to tweak the process and I also make a note while I'm doing the third version whether I actually like making it. Sometimes I never go past the third version eg the handbag inner (see pic) My friend had shown me her new (awful) lime green nylon version she had bought at the airport (you're supposed to put all the contents from your handbag into this and then when you change your handbag, you just lift this whole thing out of one bag and put it in another. I had a look at it, and what it was supposed to do, and then came up with my version and did it in my Country Girl Corner colours and though it looked quite nice.
I moved onto version 2 and improved the side pockets and added a little more decoration, and then got down to version 3 and decided I never wanted to make another one of these EVER. Don't know why, just didn't enjoy it, didn't really see the point (not all my bags are the same size, and I only really change my bag winter/summer or big for small)
so I didn't really have the need. So version 1 went in the bin, version 2 was given to my friend, and I kept version 3 for my records.

Country Girl Corner

Magnets and pegs

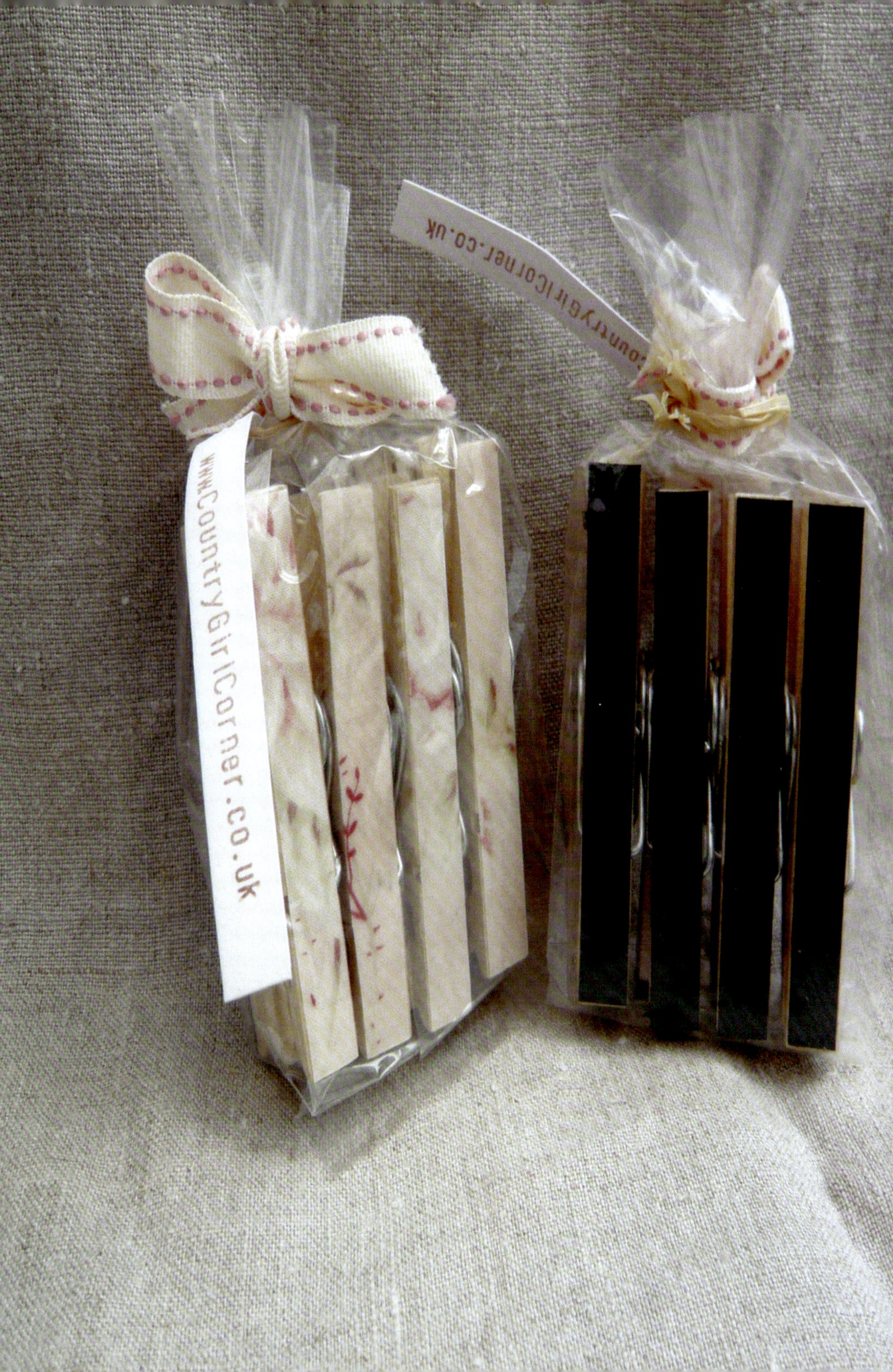
www.CountryGirlCorner.co.uk

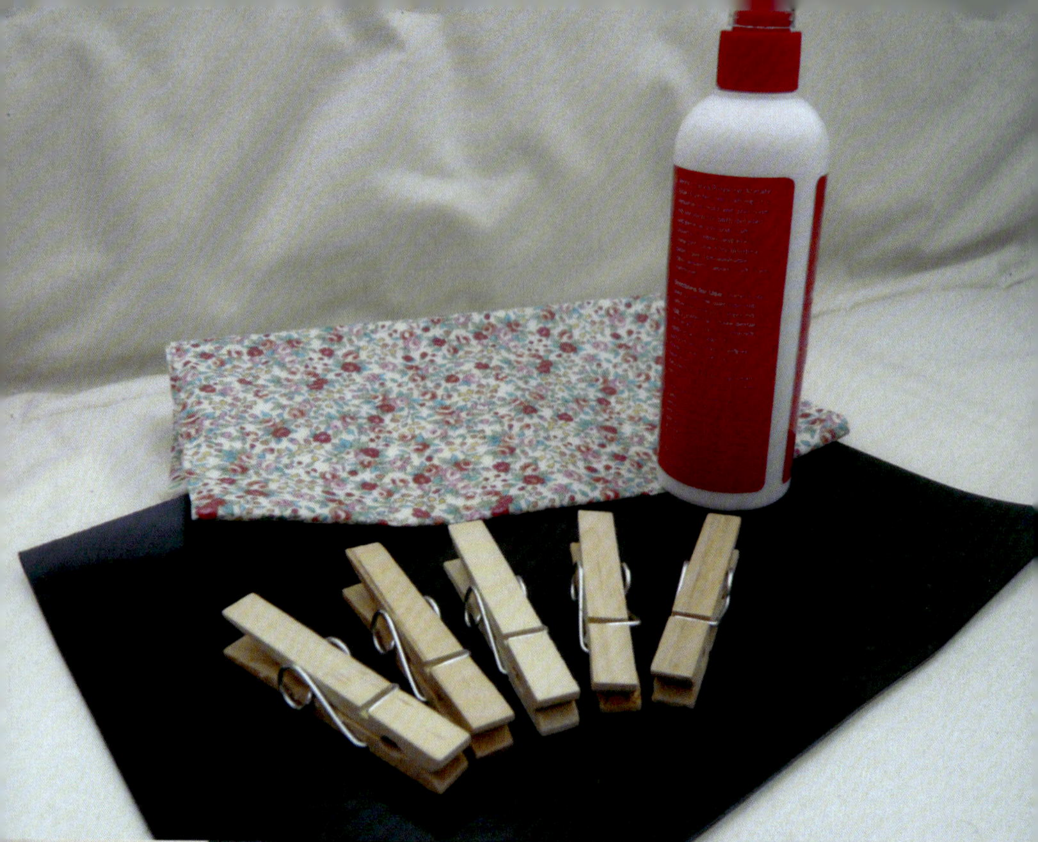

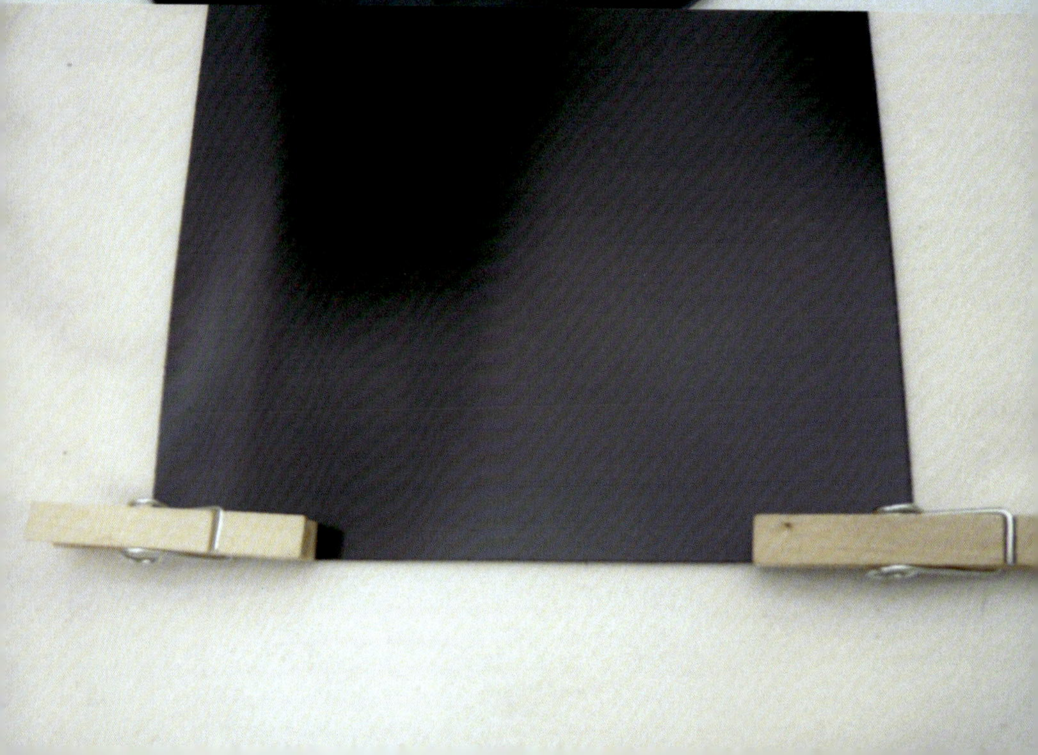

Magnets & Pegs

You will need:

Packet of wooden clothes pegs
magnetic sheet 1-2 mm thick (1/16")
piece of oilcloth fabric
glue

Firstly take your magnetic sheet and stick it on the fridge door to work out which is the magnetic side (oh yes!)

Take two pegs and place at either side of magnetic sheet and draw a line across.
Cut along line to cut strips
do the same with the oilcloth
To make a nice presentation pack four pegs should have a magnet on one side, and cloth on the other
The other four pegs should have cloth on both sides

You can cut the strips into approximate lengths slightly larger than the length of the pegs

Glue the relevant piece to each side of the pegs and when the glue has dried you can trim to neaten

You can package these in bags and tie a contrasting ribbon around the top and these make fantastic presents

Colourful cushions

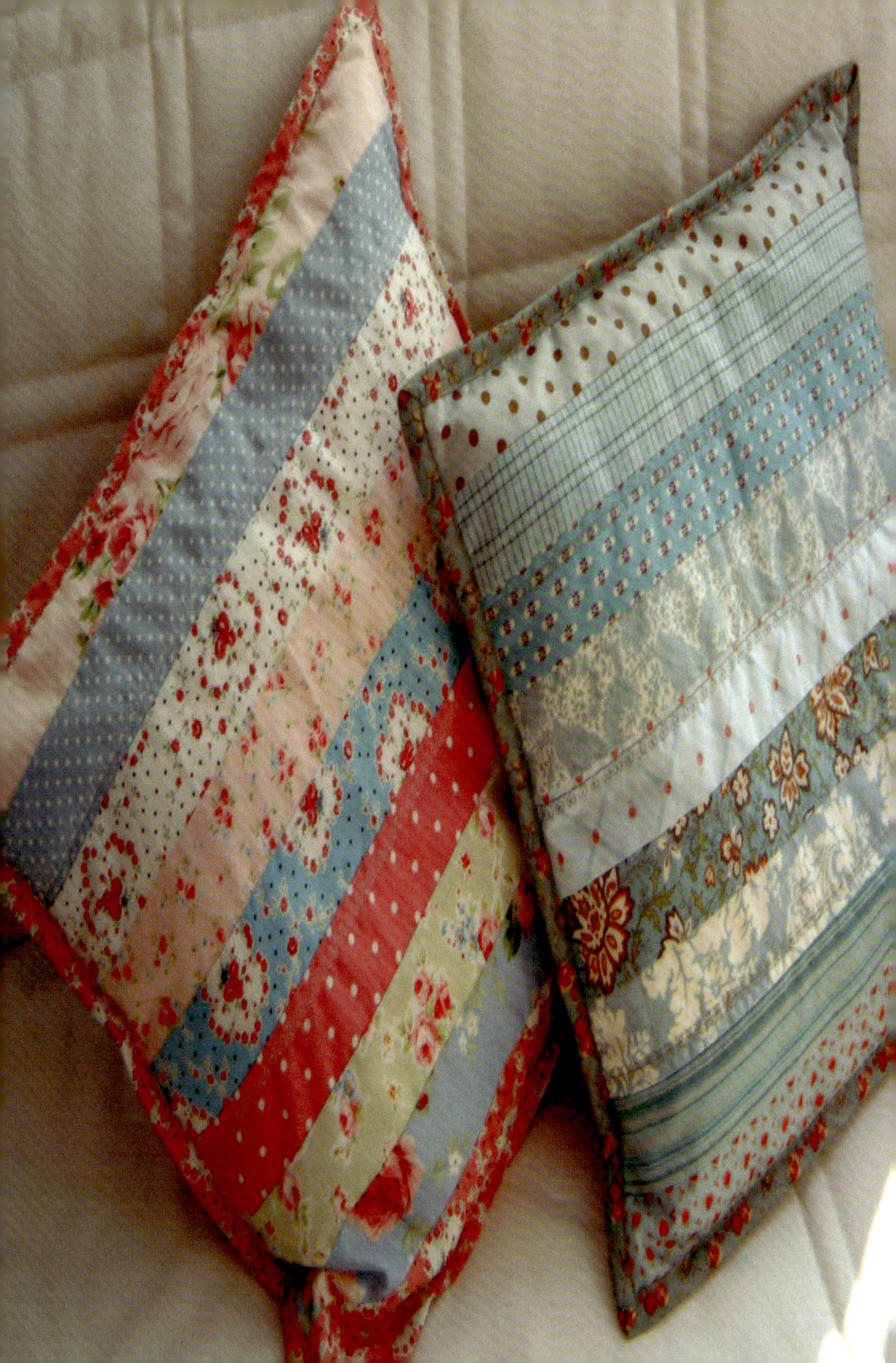

Cushion Cover

You will need:

Cushion pad 45cm (18")
11 strips contrasting fabric 5cm x 45cm (2" x 18")
2 x linen pieces 45cm x 30cm (18" x 12")

Lay the strips side by side and sew them together. For the back hem one of the long sides of each of the pieces. These pieces will overlap at the back and should then be the same size as the top piece. The easiest way of making the cushions is to lay the two linen pieces on top of one another (right sides up) overlapping the hemmed edges, and then lay the striped piece on top (right sides down). Pin and sew around the four sides, turn to the right side out and insert the cushion pad.

Alternatively you can lay down your striped piece (right side down), followed by your two back panels (right side up), pin the pieces together and sew around close to the edge. Then either cut a strip of contrasting fabric 4cm (1 1/2") wide and long enough to go around all four sides, or use bias binding and starting half way along one side on the front, pin the strip right sides together around the four edges and sew in place, then take the strip over the edge of the cushion over to the back, fold in a hem and hand stitch the binding to the back of the cushion. Trim the two ends of the binding so they overlap by 2cm (1/2"), turn over the raw edges and hand stitch closed. Insert the cushion pad.

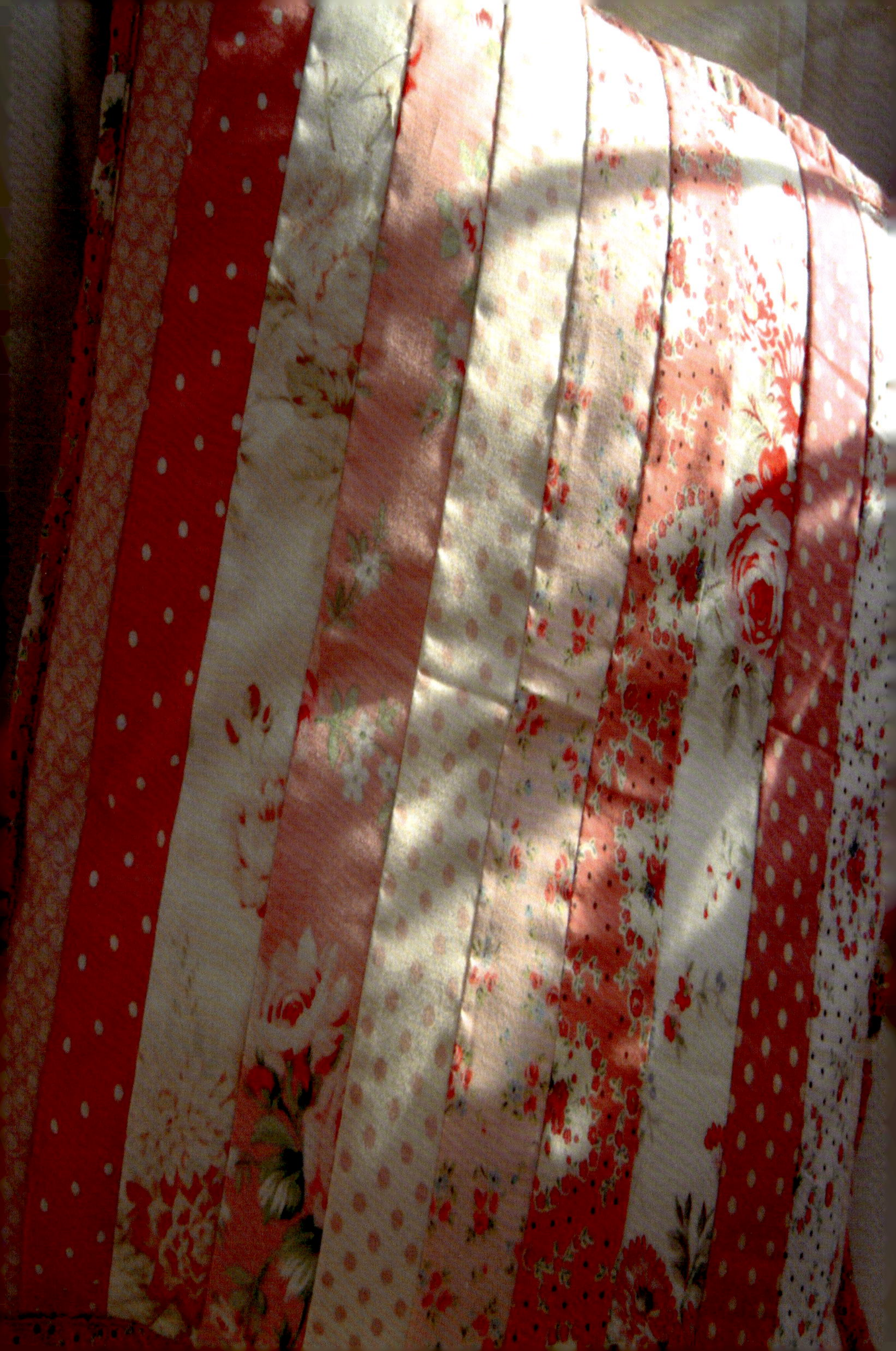

Lap quilt
(using charm packs)

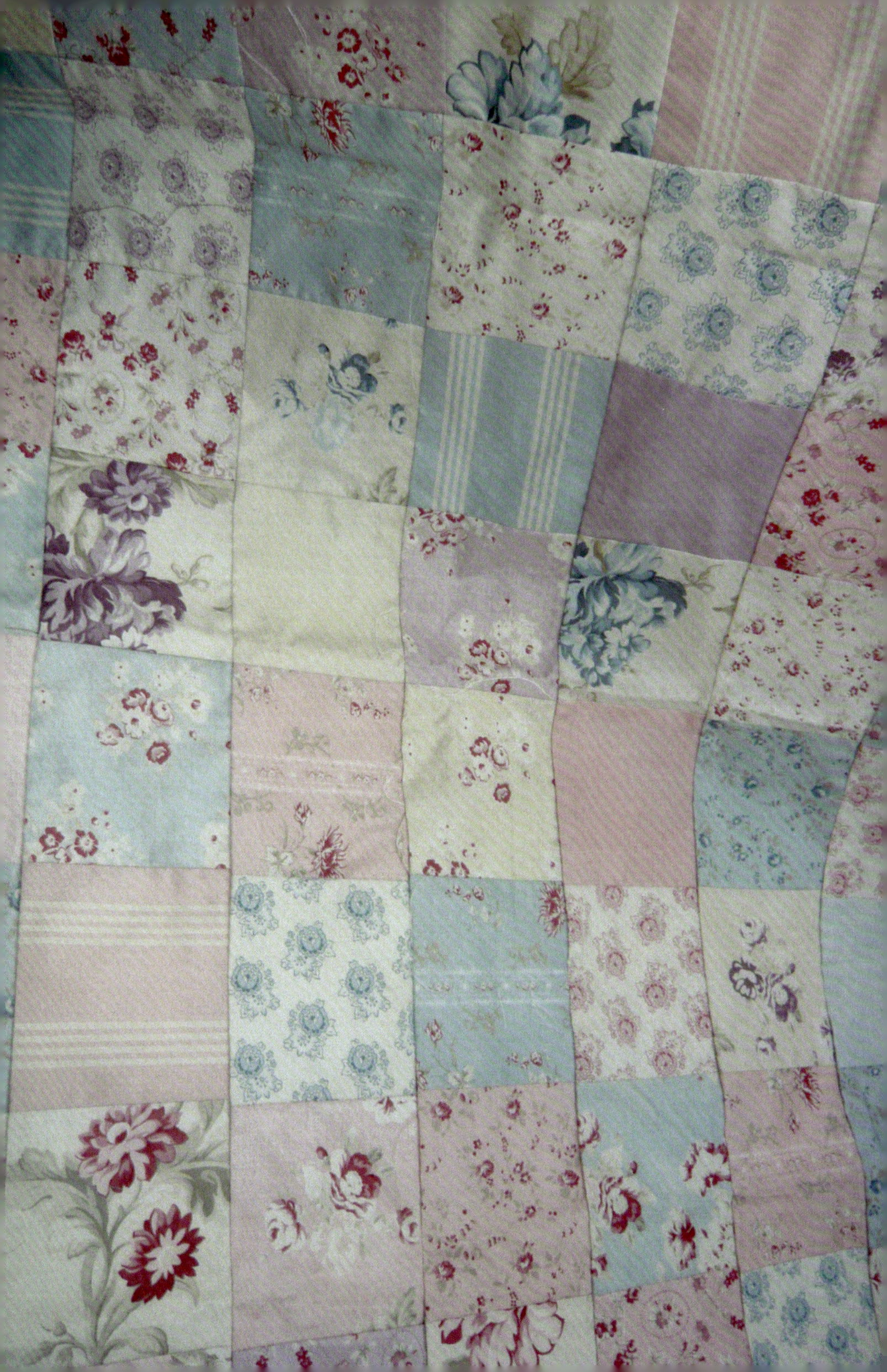

Lap Quilt

You will need:
2 x charm packs assorted fabric
1 x coloured single flat sheet
wadding
(Manufacturers produce charm packs
for each of their new ranges, these
are a mix of squares 12cm x 12cm (5" x 5")
(see Etsy or Ebay for charm packs)

Lay out the squares in 6 rows of 5, arrange them so the colours and patterns are evenly spread. Sew the squares together one strip at a time, and then sew the strips together. Iron the piece at this stage and get all the raw edges at the back to lie flat. Take your sheet and from one end width ways, cut strips 10cm (3") wide and long enough to sew one strip to the top and bottom of your square panel, and then to sew a strip down each side. Sew the border.

Using your complete patchwork piece top, cut out a piece of wadding and the backing sheet slightly bigger than your 'top' piece.

Lay down your wadding first, then your backing fabric (right side up), followed by your patchwork piece (right side down) and pin around the sides.
Sew around each side leaving an opening approx 20cm (10") at one end, and then turn the quilt through (between the patchwork and backing fabric layer) which will then have the wadding sandwiched in the middle. Slip stitch over the open edge to close. You can sew a running stitch around 'in the ditch' ie where the patchwork fabrics are joined. (you can even use a contrasting thread)

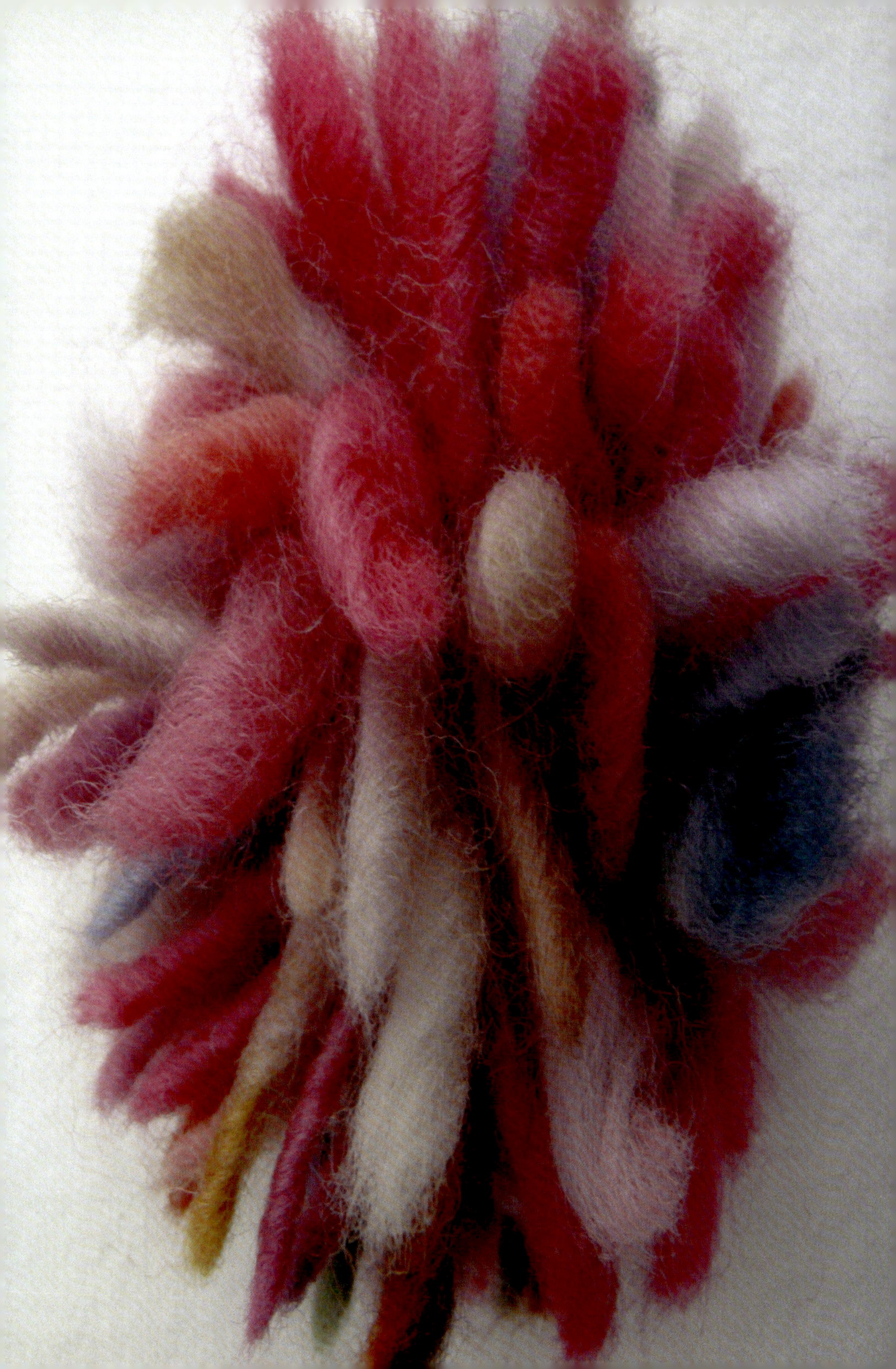

Fuzzy Brooch

You will need

1m (1 yd) thick wool or yarn or strip of
fabric 1cm (1/4") wide
1 large brooch back the type that
has 3 holes in the frame

Hold a 10cm (4") tail between your fingers, and
start wrapping the rest of the wool loosely
around your other 4 fingers.

Hold onto the wool and take your fingers out and
wrap the end around the middle of your wrap a
few times and then tie the two loose ends
together tightly

With matching thread sew the large brooch back onto
the centre back of your wrap (also sew the thread
all the way through the centre a few times
just to secure all the pieces in place

Once the brooch back is secured, then (and only
then), take your scissors and cut the loops at
both sides. Holding the brooch back, give
the thing a good shake and then start
trimming....

You are aiming at an even dome shape -
so don't get carried away

Fuzzy brooch

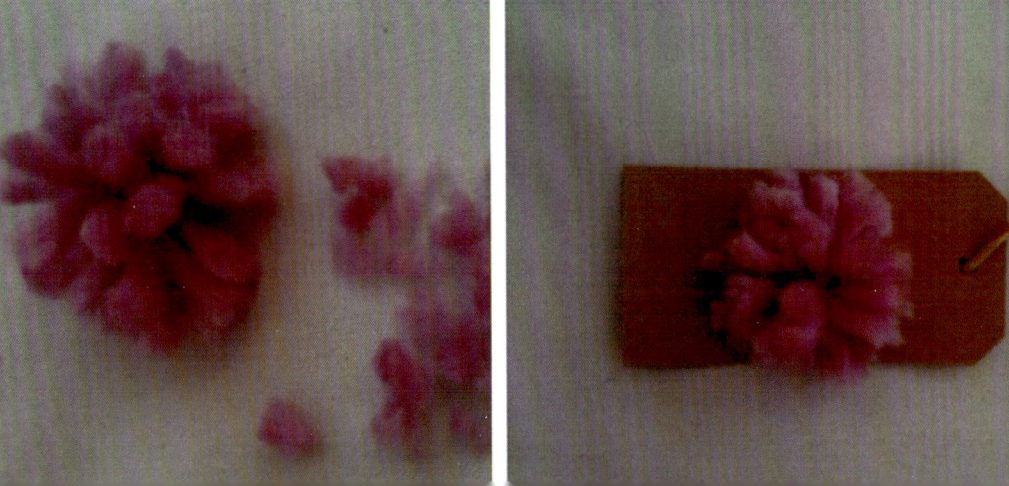

Rose quartz bracelet

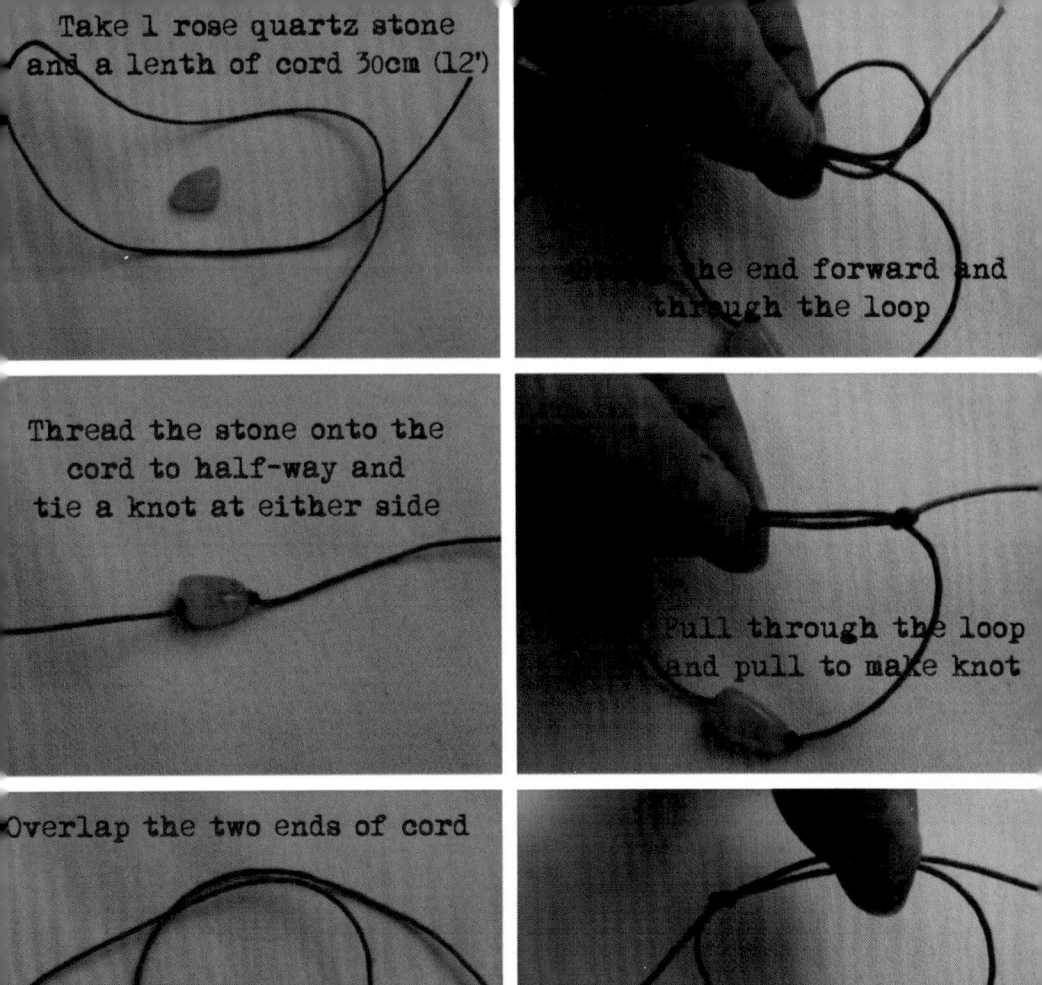

Take 1 rose quartz stone and a lenth of cord 30cm (12")	Bring the end forward and through the loop
Thread the stone onto the cord to half-way and tie a knot at either side	Pull through the loop and pull to make knot
Overlap the two ends of cord	Turn bracelet around and repeat on other side
With one end, make a loop and bring the end behind	Tie knots on the loose end and cut excess off

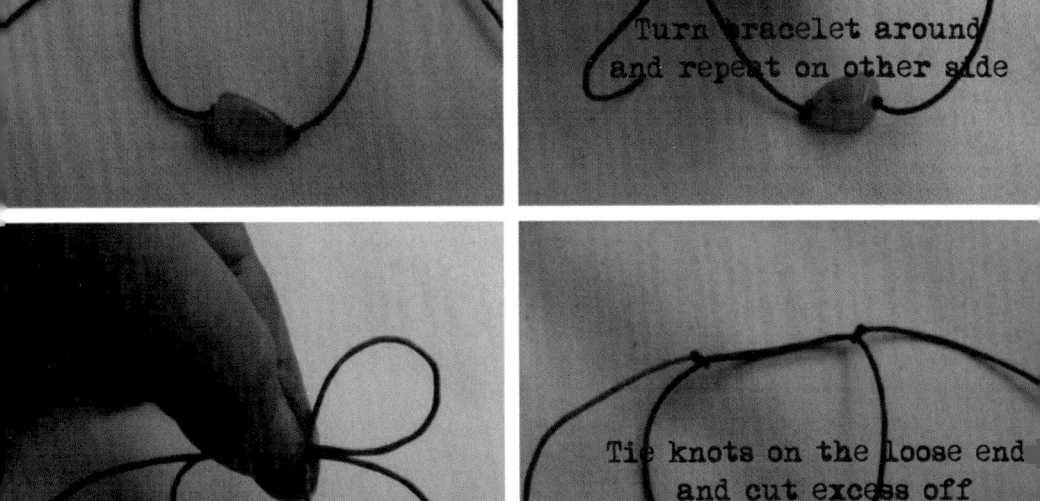

Liberty Bracelet

You Will Need

    a strip of fabric 1cm x 30 cm (1/4" x 12")
selection of beads and charms (these need to have large holes)

Tie a knot in one end of the fabric and hold tightly with one hand and twist and twist the length of the fabric until it all curls in on itself and tie it around a mug (still with the twists in) spray with water and then leave to dry (this helps to hold the twists in place). Once dry, untie from the mug, and thread on the beads and charms and then tie a knot at the other end so you have a knot at each end to prevent the beads falling off.....
tie around your wrist for a lovely boho look

Liberty Bracelet

Spring Rose Brooch

You will need

a piece of fabric 30cm x 7cm (12" x 3")
1 brooch back
scrap of fabric/toy filler (something soft to pad out the centre)

Using the pattern provided, cut 6 circles for the petals, and two circles for the centre front/back. Take one 'petal' circle, fold in half to make a semi-circle, then fold in half again, sew a running stitch along the raw edges and pull tight to gather the fabric and secure the end of the thread. repeat for the remaining petals

Take two of the petals and slightly overlap at the raw edge and stitch together, then add the next petal, slightly overlap and stitch together until all the petals are joined. Gently pull the two ends together and overlap and stitch together
Take the two remaining circles and sew a running stitch around the edge and pull the thread to gather in the edges (don't pull tight, you only want to turn over an even hem around the edge)
Pin this over the raw edges of the petals in the centre of the flower and
sew around the edge to secure in place
Turn the brooch over and put a piece of toy filler in the centre to fill out the space, and then sew the other circle piece in place over the raw edges
Take the brooch back and sew to the back of the brooch securing tightly.
Cut a strip of fabric (see pattern), turn in all the edges and sew over the base of the brooch back to neaten.

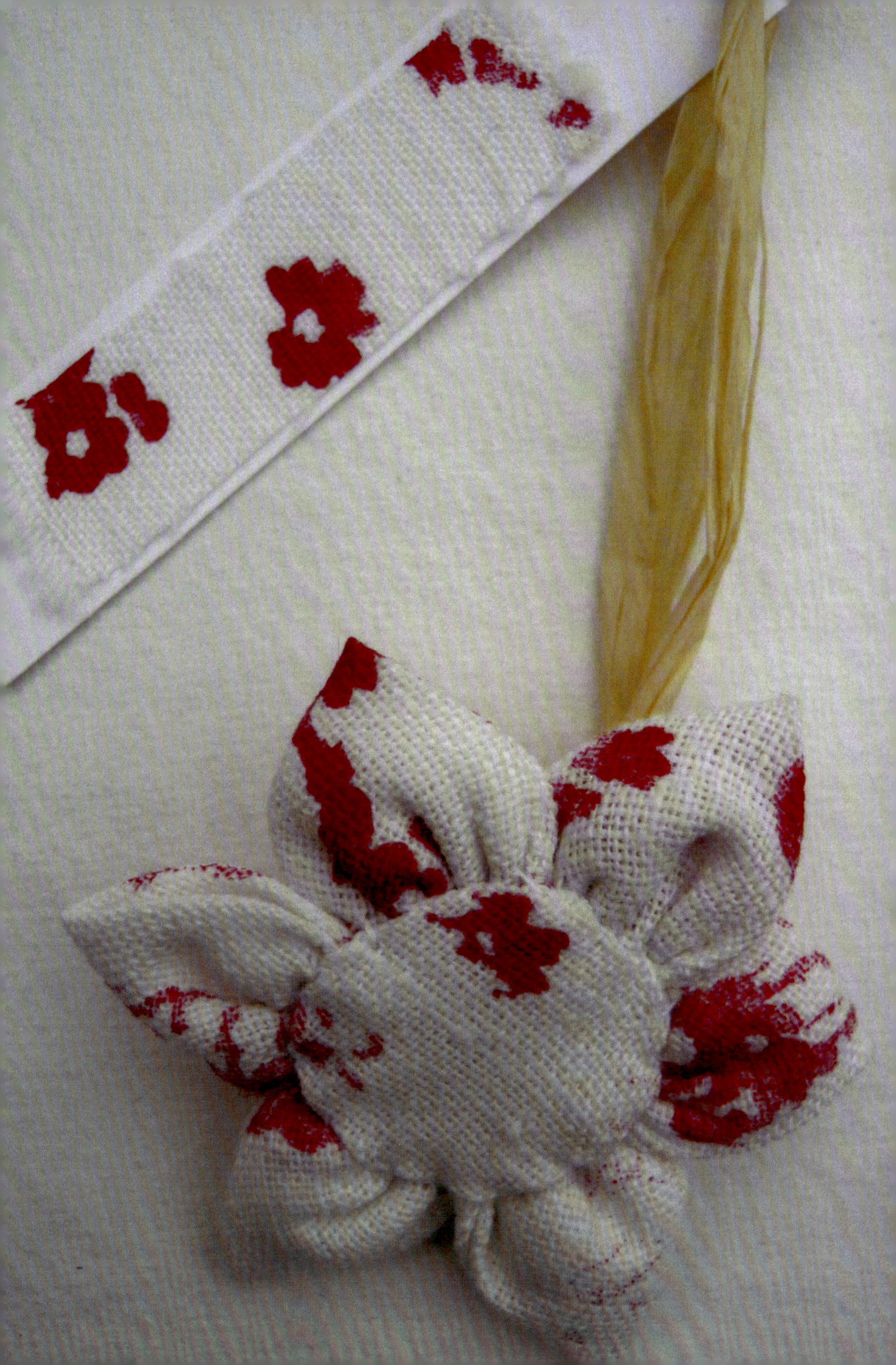

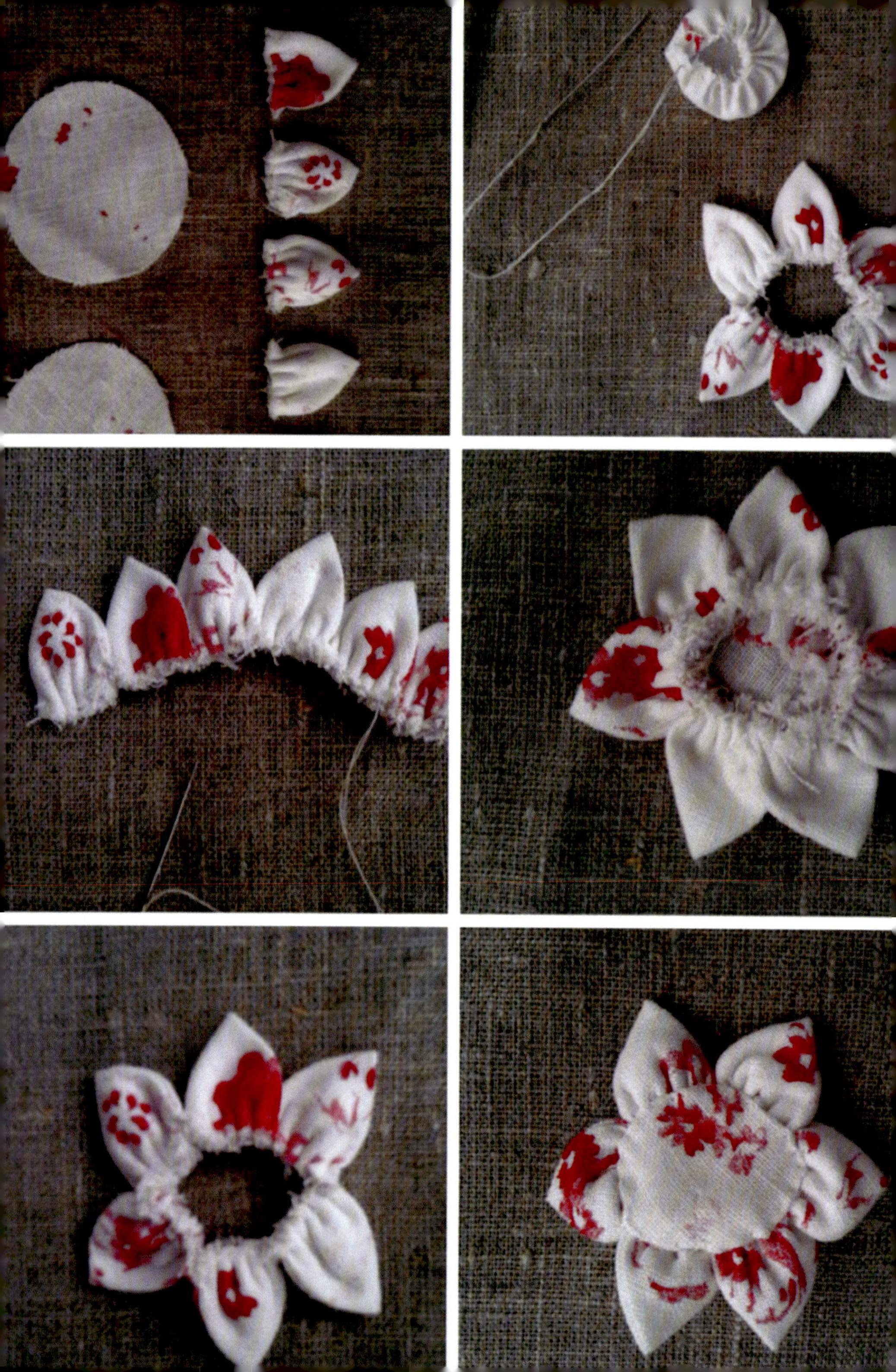

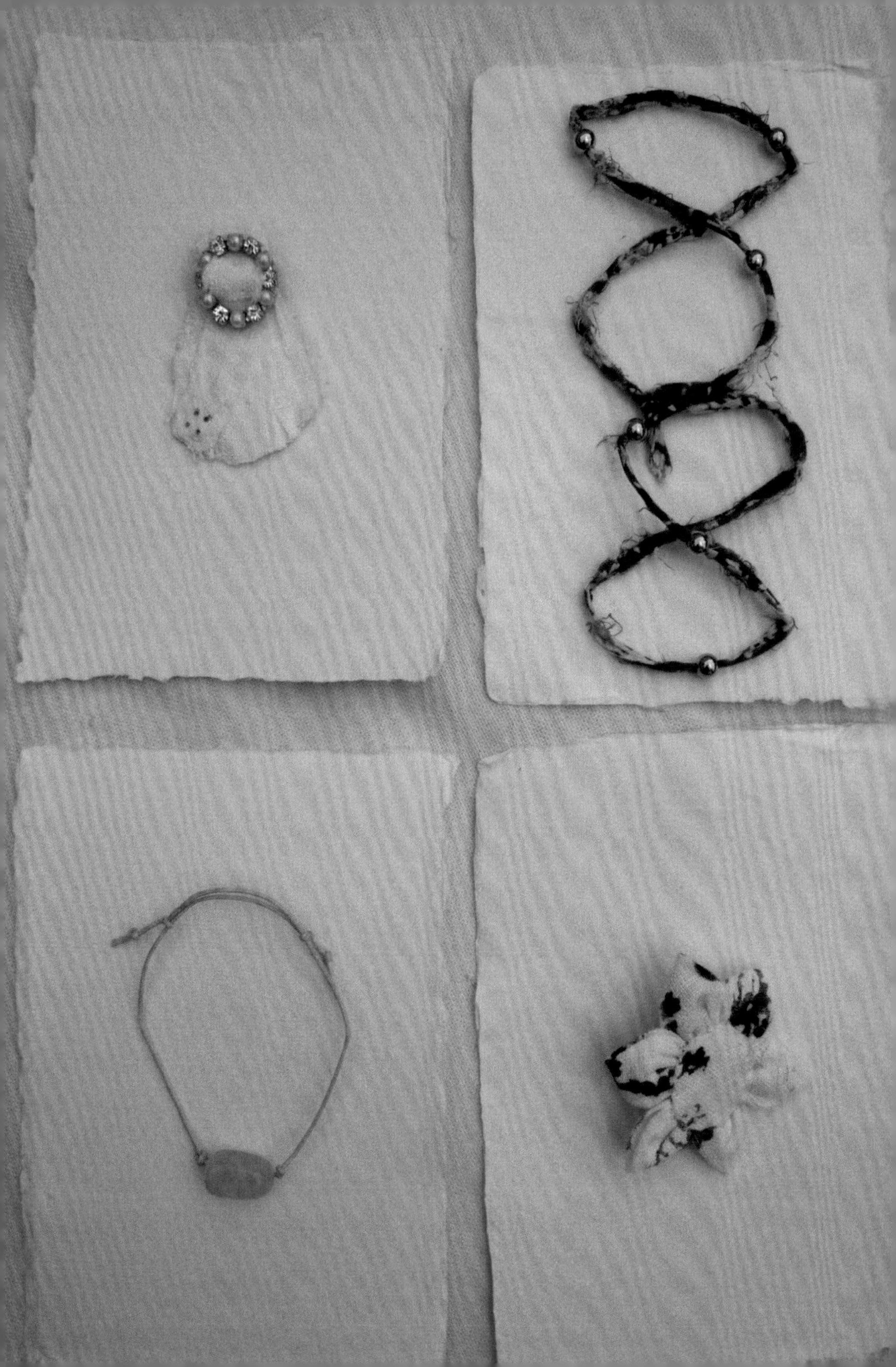

Button Necklaces

These are very easy to make
and are always commented upon as they make
really unusual necklaces.

I always have a rummage in a button box when
I see one at a car boot, and can't resist
brightly coloured buttons.

You will need
a selection of buttons and linen/waxed
cotton cord. You need to hold the thread
around your neck to gauge the length
and then double it to make sure you have allowed
enough length once all the knots are tied.
Thread the best button on
and tie in the middle of the thread (use
the best button as this will be your
main feature button which will sit at the front).
Then proceed to thread your
buttons on and tie knots before and after
each one to prevent them all slipping
to the front, and space them evenly
up each side from the main button in the
middle.

Tie sliding knots with the ends of the cord
to be able to adjust the length of your
necklace (see rose quartz bracelet
instructions for the sliding knot)

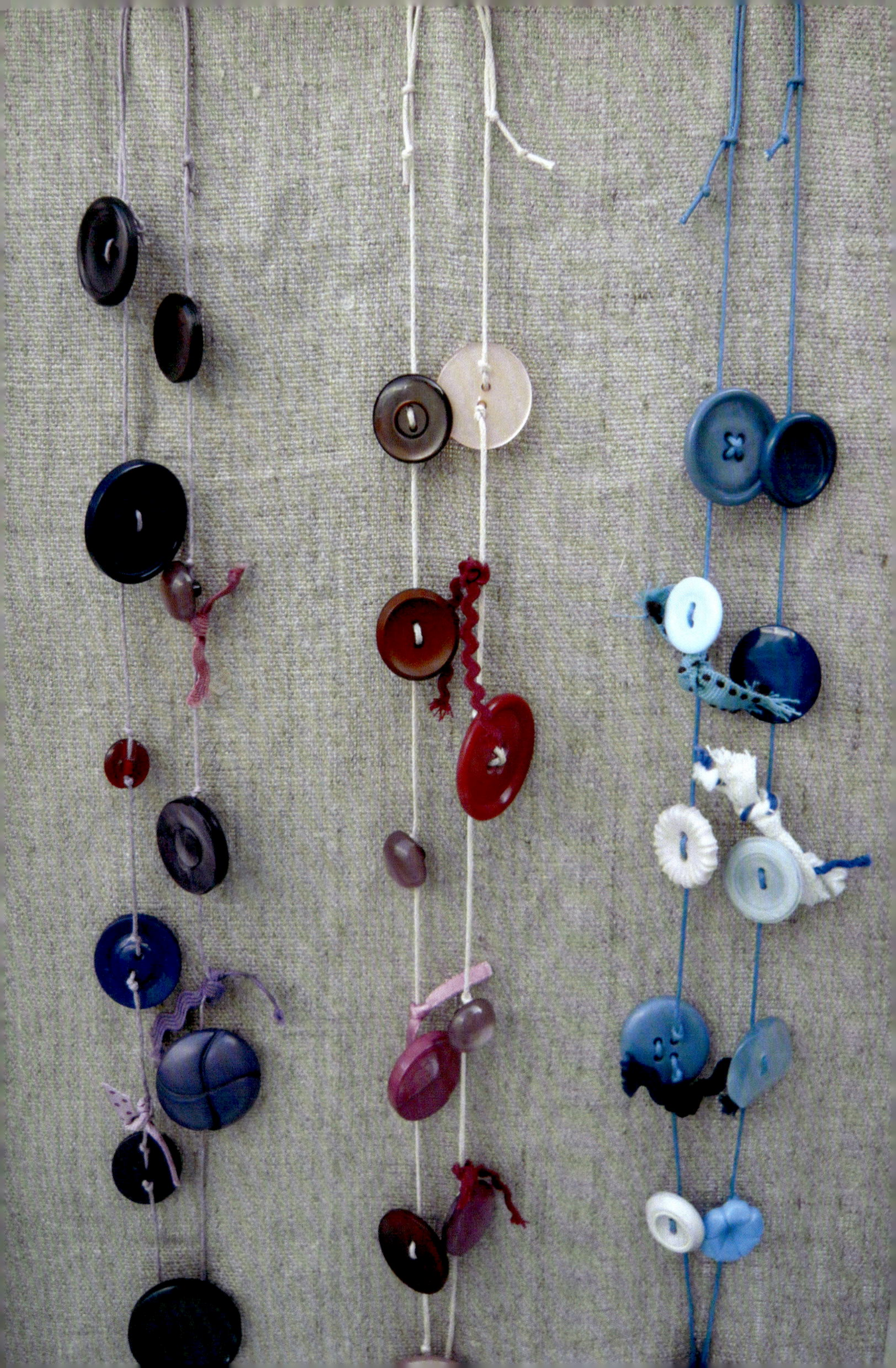

Pearl Necklace

You will need:

14 freshwater pearls (drilled)
14 silver head pins (get the fine ones because you need to make sure they will fit through the holes in the pearls
strong linen thread/waxed linen thread/ threading cord
pliers & tweezers & wire cutters

Put the head pin through 1 of the pearls and hold the wire just above the pearl with the tweezers, and with the pliers twist the wire around until you have made a loop

Hold the top of the loop with the tweezers and twist the wire around the top of the pearl a few times to secure (cut off the end of the headpin and squeeze the end in amongst the twists to cover any sharp ends.

(repeat for the other 11 pearls)

Thread two pearls onto your cord and tie a knot to secure them at the halfway point. Continue up each side, tying a pearl approx two fingers width apart (you should have two in the middle and 5 up each side)

Overlap the ends of the cord and tie an adjustable knot, (see pattern for rose quartz bracelet), thread the remaining pearls on the loose ends and tie a knot to secure in place.

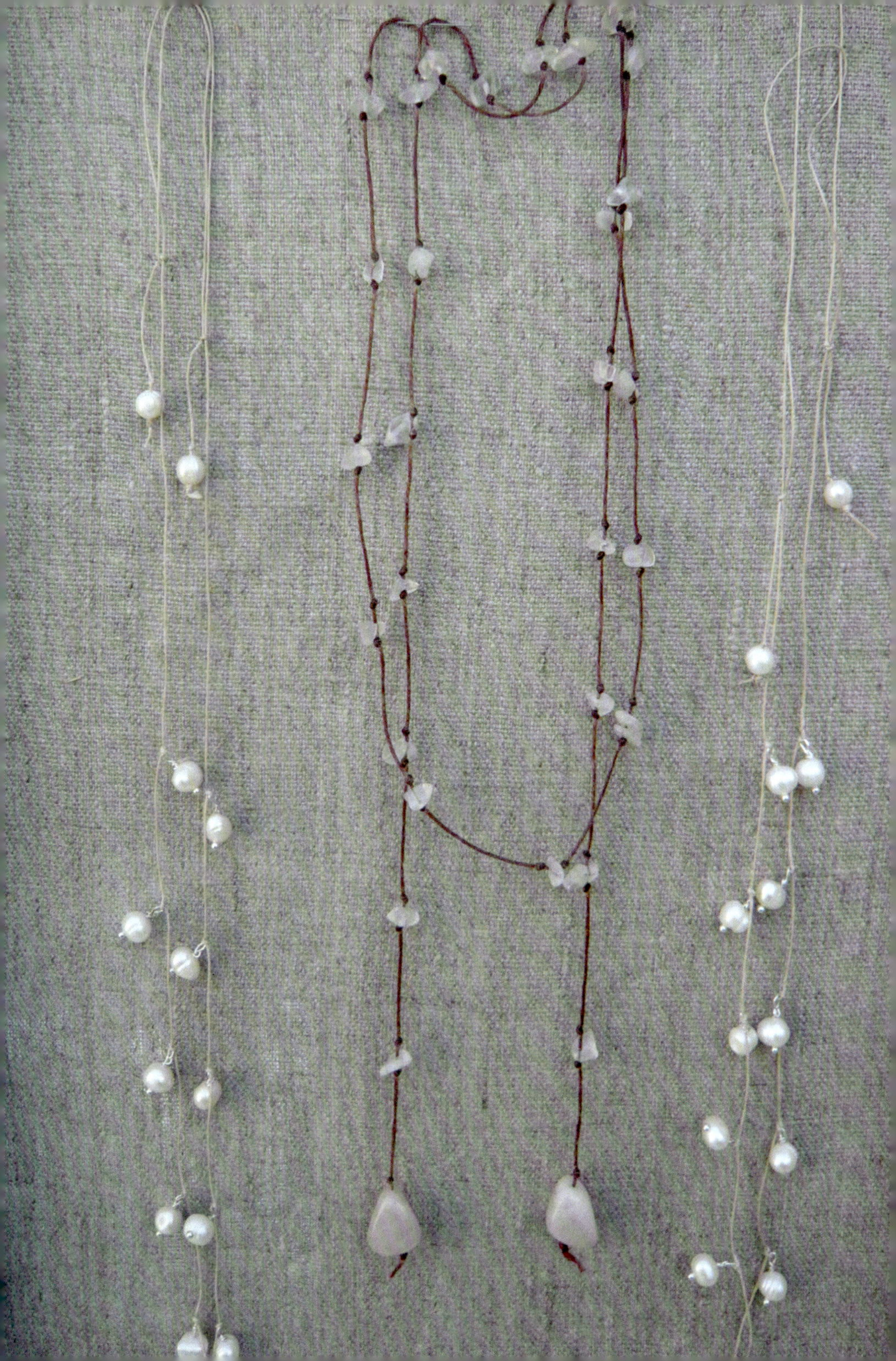

Amethyst Lariat

You will need:

1.5m (60") waxed linen cord (unwaxed work just as well)
Chipped amethyst bracelet - these are normally threaded on elastic thread and there are lots of irregular pieces of chipped amethyst/rose quartz etc
2 larger drilled stones 1-2 cm

Cut the bracelet carefully over a bowl to separate the pieces of amethyst. Thread one of the pieces onto your cord to the half way point and tie a knot on either side of the stone to keep it in place. Continue up each side of the cord spacing the knot/stone/knot combination approx 2 fingers width distance apart.
When you have around 1m (40") of cord threaded with chipped stones, then tie your larger stones one at each end. Tie a few knots at the end of the larger stones to ensure they are secure.

Wrap loosely once around your neck and leave the two ends dangling....

or thread through the belt loops of jeans and use as a decorational belt

Country

Activity bag

You will need

1 piece chalkboard fabric 18cm x 18cm (7" x 7")
fat quarter coloured fabric and calico
(chalk board fabric available on Etsy)
cut front and back pieces (24cm x 24cm) (10" x 10")
plus coloured straps as long as your
fabric will allow

optional chalk bag 25cm x 12cm (10" x 5")
(fold in half right sides together, sew
around three sides, turn to right side
and turn in the top edge and sew a
running stitch around to create a
channel - thread through ribbon and
tie to strap of bag

Cut out the pieces

Sew the chalkboard fabric to the front

Straps: fold long strips in half lenthways, turn in raw edges and sew down seam

Pin the straps to the front and the back....

Sew a lining piece to the top edge of the front & back pieces

Open out and put together right sides together

Start at * sew down side/bottom and up other side

Turn right side out through the open lining end

Turn in the open lining edge and sew across, then push down into body of bag

Denim bags

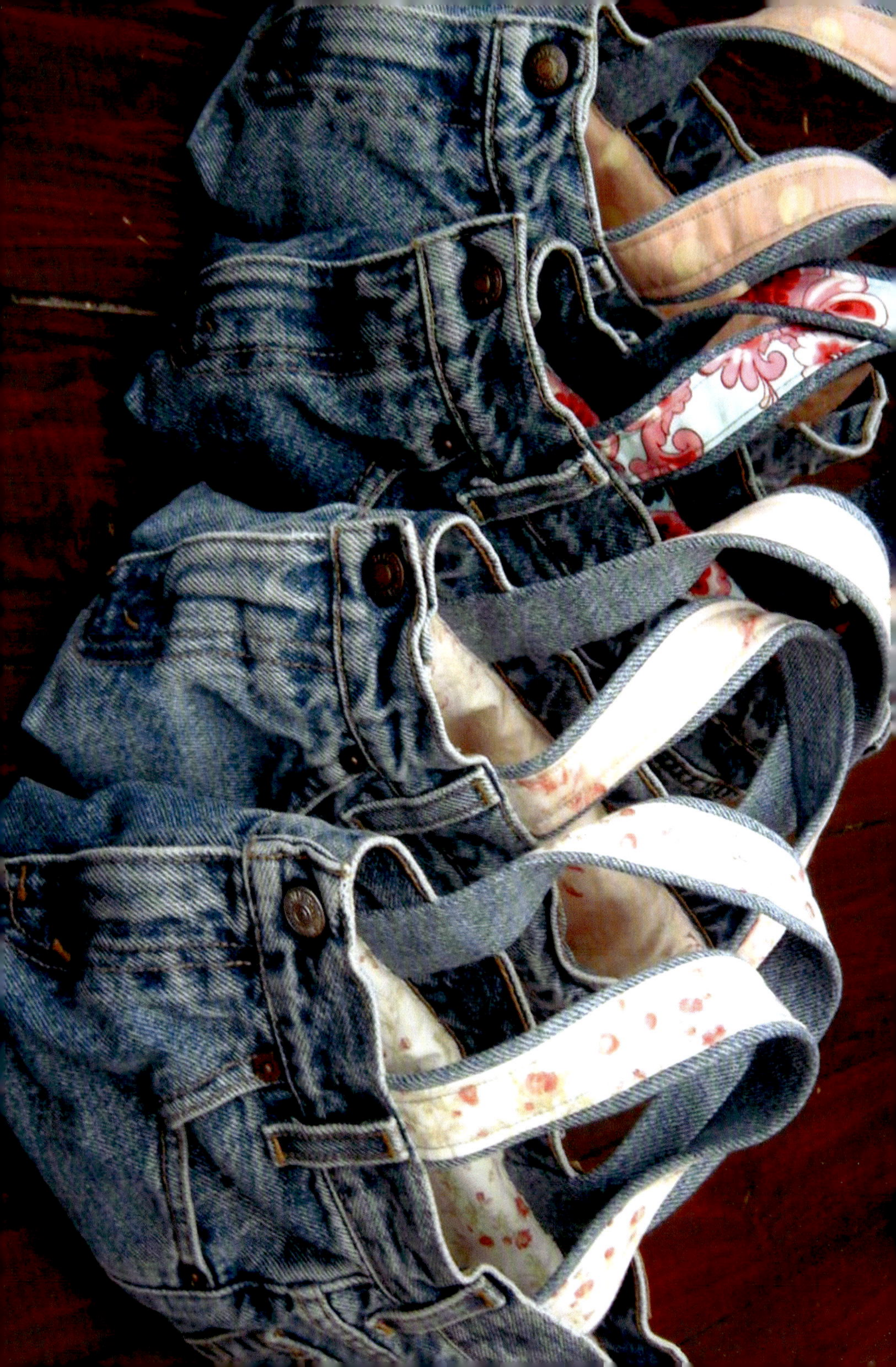

Denim Bags

You will need
1 pair jeans (waist 26" or 28")
1/2m (1/2 yd) fabric
1/2m (1/2 yd) wadding

Cut the legs off the jeans approx 10cm (4") down the leg from the crotch (make sure you don't cut the bottom of the pockets off). Cut the seam between the legs to open up. Turn inside out. Lay flat with the front zip at one side and the back seam at the other side. Sew a line across the bottom edge approx 2-3cm (1") from the bottom edge. Open the jeans and push the front zip inside of the bag so it is lying on the inside of the newly sewn line, Flatten the fabric at the front and sew across (see dia), repeat at the back, turn to right side. Cut 2 strips from the back of one of the legs, 6cm x 50cm (2 1/2" x 20") and put to one side - these will be part of the straps.

To make the lining, you need to fold your fabric in half (right sides together), the depth needs to reach from the top of the waistband to the sewn line across the bottom of the bag, the width needs to be the width of the waistband from the front zip to the back seam. So, fold your fabric and lay the jeans on top, mark the width of the bag, then you need to cut two more strips (still with the fold in the fabric) which will be needed for the straps, and one additional piece which will be the lining end pieces. Cut a piece of wadding the same size as the main lining piece and sew it to the wrong side of the main lining piece, one line across the middle and one at each end. Then take the lining end strip, and cut it in half and sew the short ends one at each side in the middle of the main lining piece (right sides together)

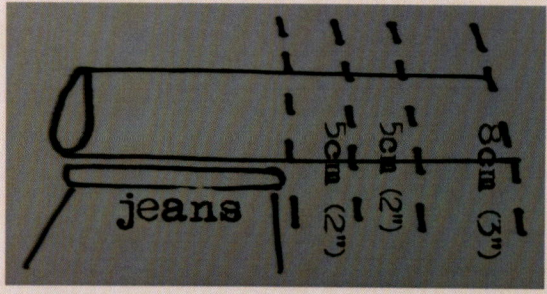

Then sew the edges to the main lining piece to create a box shape (see pic) Insert this into the inside of the jeans. Turn over 2cm (1/2") at the back and pin to the inside of the jeans below the waistband, work around until the all the lining has been pinned.
To make the straps, take one strip of denim and fold long edges to the centre seam and pin. Pin the fabric strip in the same way, and place one on top of the other to enclose all the raw edges (re-pin) and sew down each side of the fabric (see pic)
Then pin the straps in the bag between the lining nd the outer ensuring they are in the correct position and are the same length .
Then hand sew the lining to the bag (this can't be done on a sewing machine because there are too many rivets etc) When you get all the way around, then go back to each strap and starting on the inside, sew the side of the strap to the inside of the waistband, through to the outside, along the front, then back through to the inside and back down the other side of the strap to meet the lining.

I had been making denim bags for a while and sourced a man who could supply children's jeans, so we made the arrangements and he was going to ship a boxful over to me. He contacted me again because the box was heavier than anticipated and it had tilted over into the next price bracket and he wanted to know if it was still OK to ship. I thought about it for a while and then asked him if he could cut one leg off each of the pairs of jeans, and try again with the shipping. It was below the threshold, and the jeans duly arrived. About a month later, I had an e-mail from the man saying he could resist no longer, and it had been a dinner party conversation on a number of occasions, 'what on earth did I want 50 pairs of children's jeans with only one leg'...
He laughed when I told him.

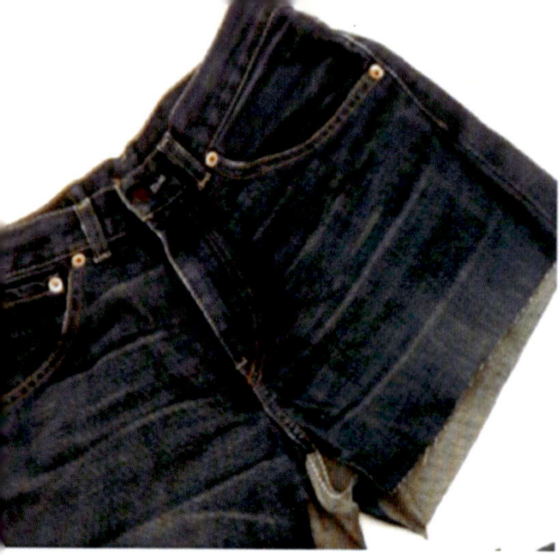
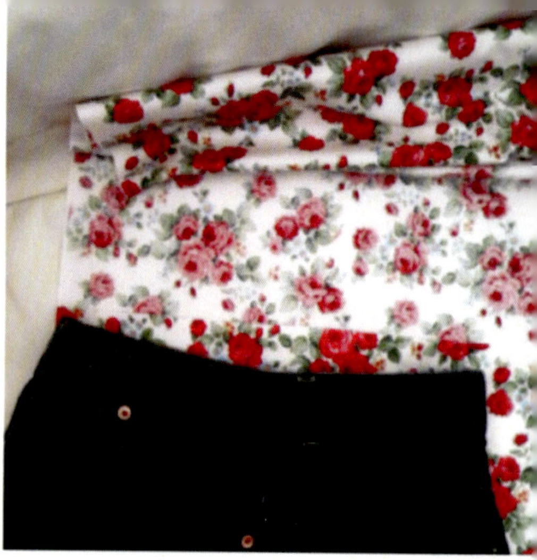
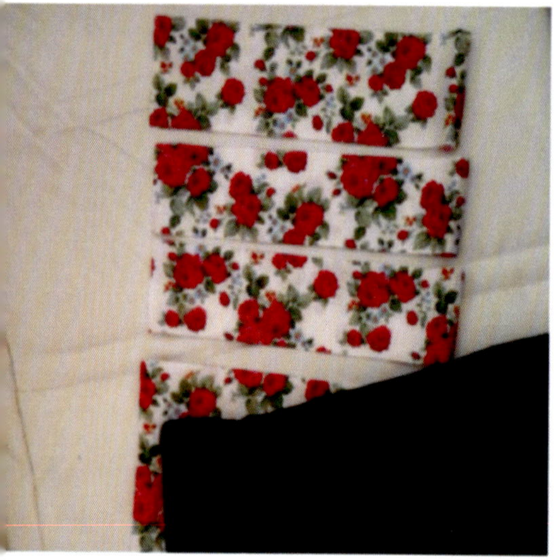
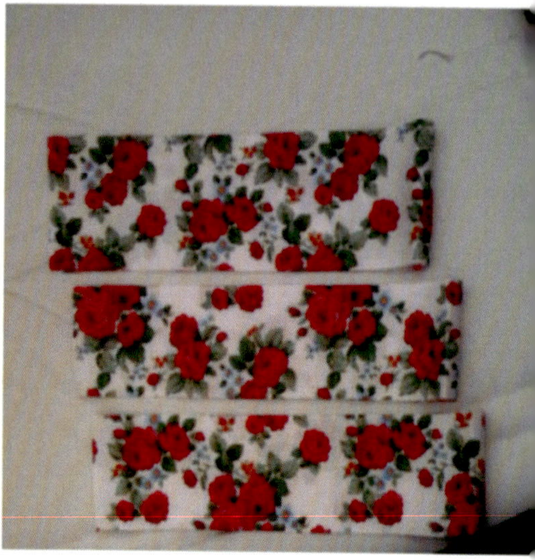
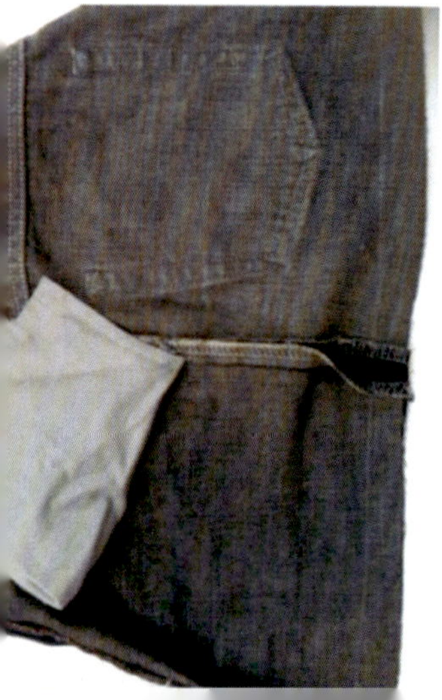
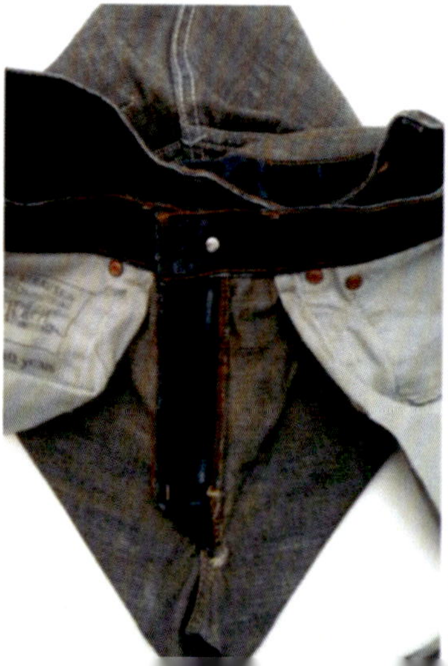
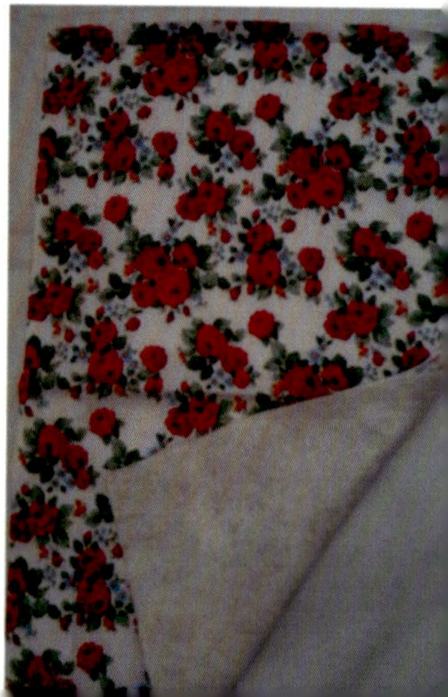

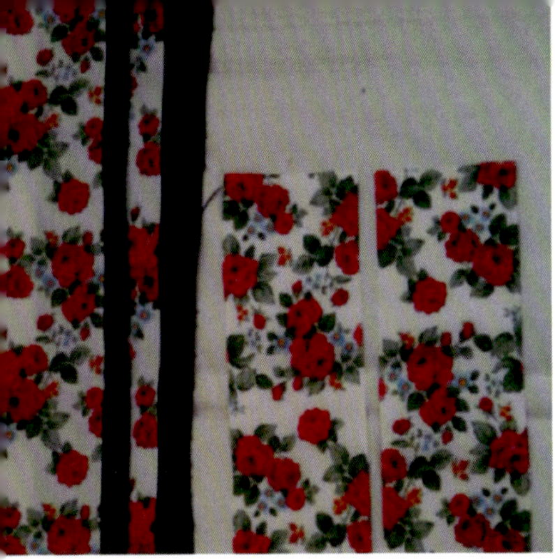
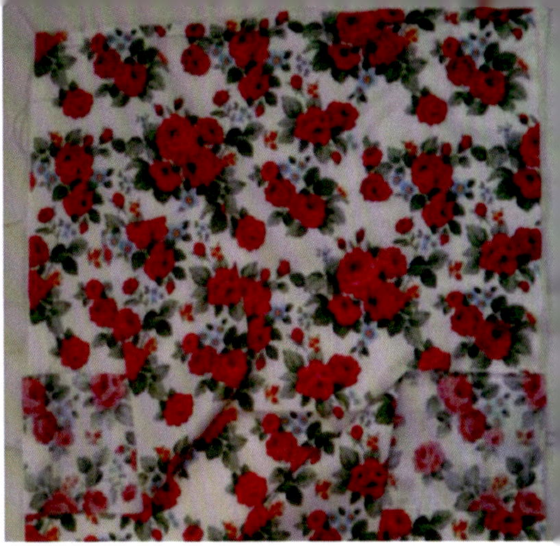
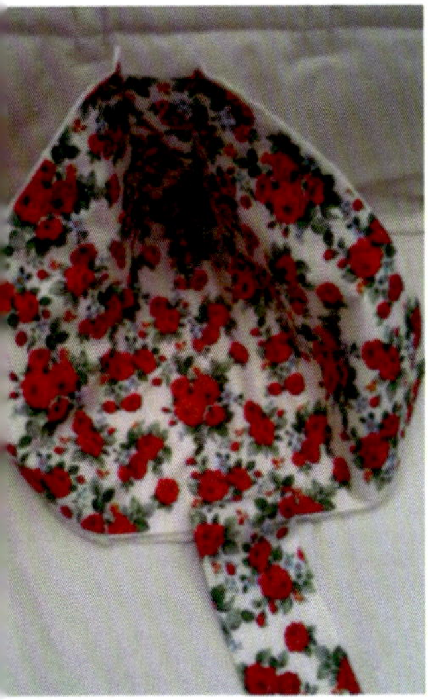
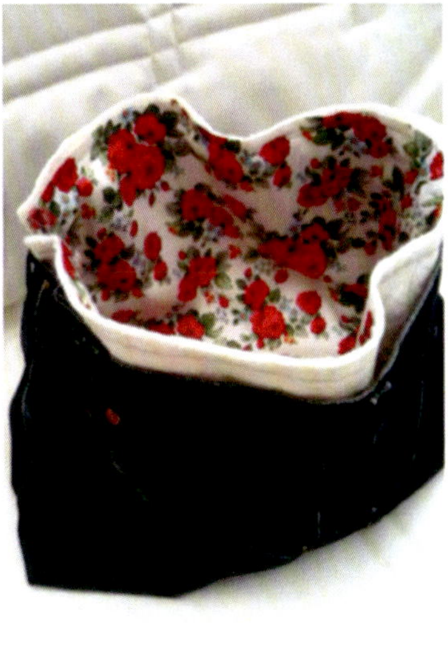
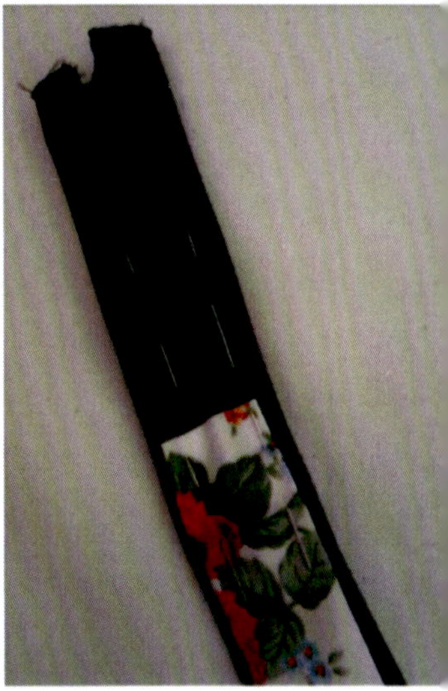
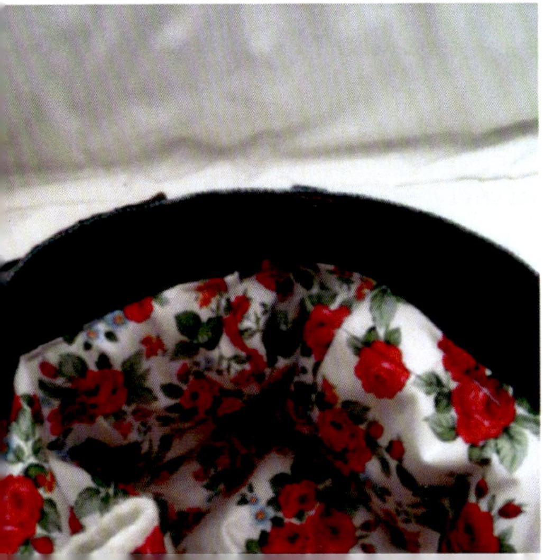
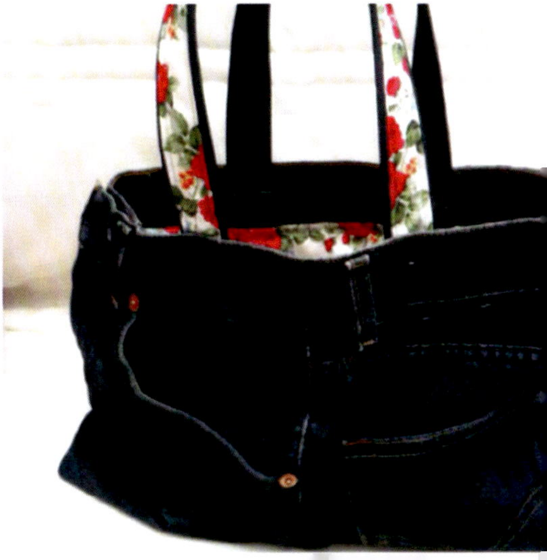

Notebook Cover

Notebook Cover

You will need

1 hard backed notebook (any size)
piece linen long enough to go around book and be tucked inside the front & back cover
floral fabric long enough to go around the book
lace trim same length as the floral fabric

You need a strip of linen which is 4cm (1 1/2") taller than your notebook (2cm (1") at the top and 2cm (1") at the bottom).
Open your book up and cut the main section 2cm (1") wider than the open book, (be careful you have allowed enough for the spine) You will then need two additional pieces which should be the width of the front of the book (one will be for the inside front cover/one for the inside back cover) These should also be 4cm taller than the book. Hem one long edge on each of these pieces.
Cut your floral fabric the same width but half the height of the main panel, the lace trim should be the same length as the width of the main panel. Match up the bottom edges of the main panel and floral strip, then turn in 1cm (1/2")along the top edge of the floral strip and carefully tuck in the lace trim and pin in place. Sew across ensuring the lace trim has been 'caught' by the machine. Take your other two pieces and with right sides together match up the raw edges at each side, pin in place (see pic) At this stage set your open book in place and check it is the correct size, tuck the front cover under the flap on the left hand side, and the back cover under the flap at the right hand side and holding everything, close the book and ensure it fits nicely. Then sew the flaps to the sides of the main panel. Re-insert the book and pin at the top and bottom edge of the book at the front and the back. Don't pin too closely to the edge of the book, you need to leave a little bit of room for the seams once the cover has been turned to the right side, Sew in place, double stitching at the edges to strengthen. Turn to right side, and turn in the edge between the flaps and zig-zag stitch over the raw edges to secure. Re-insert your book.

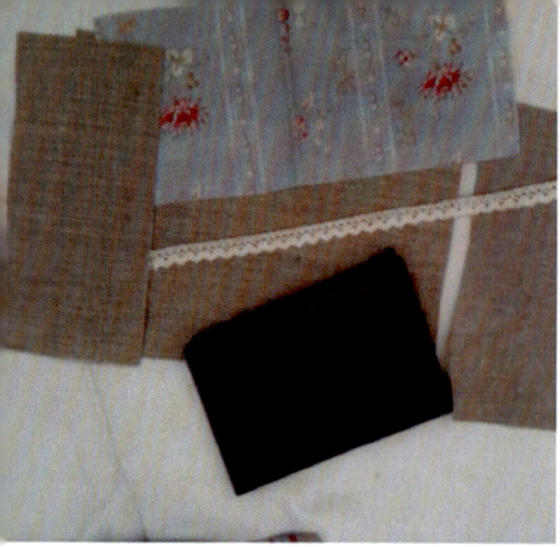
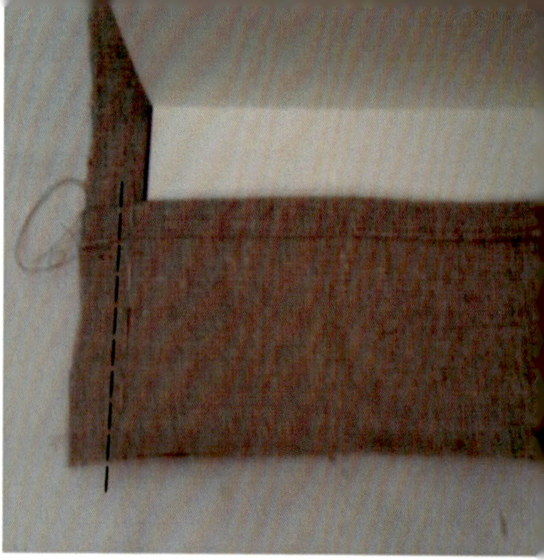
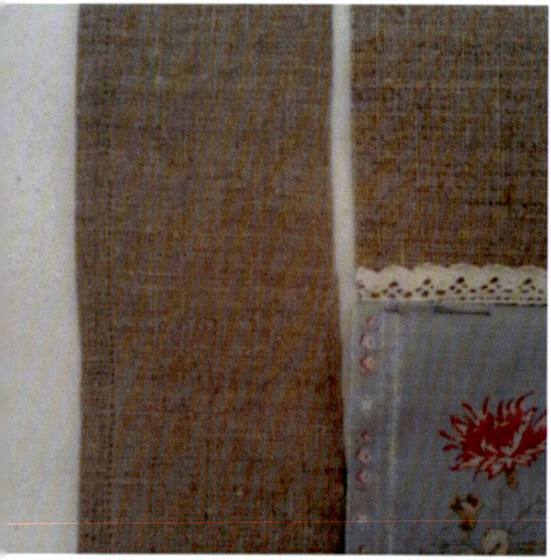
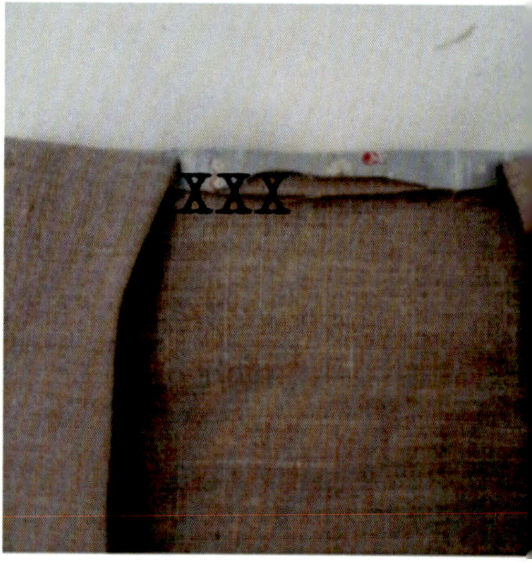
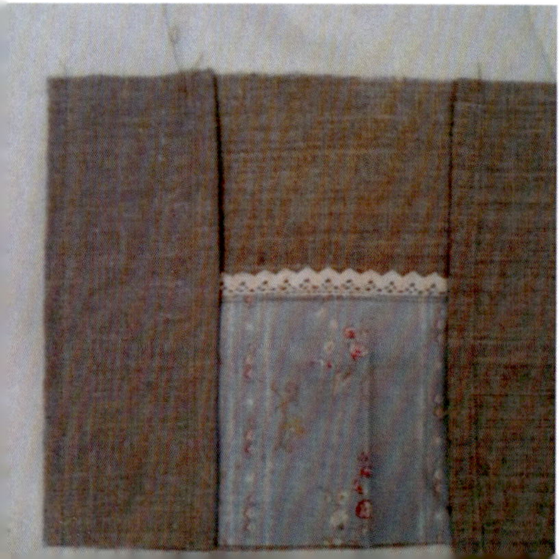
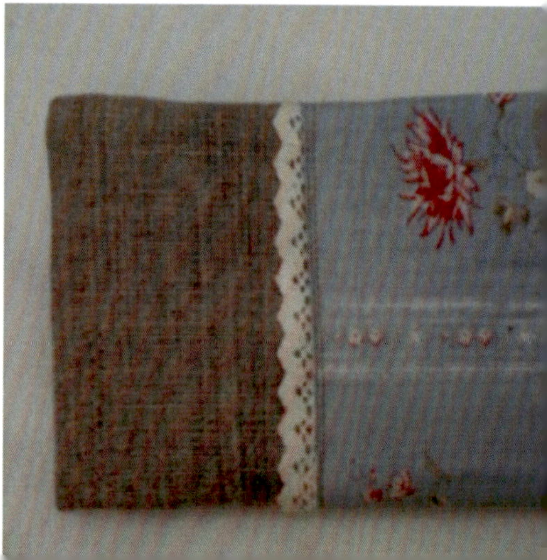

ryGirlCorner.co.uk
ryGirlCorner.co.uk
ntryGirlCorner.co.uk
GirlCorner.co.uk

Shoulder Bag

100

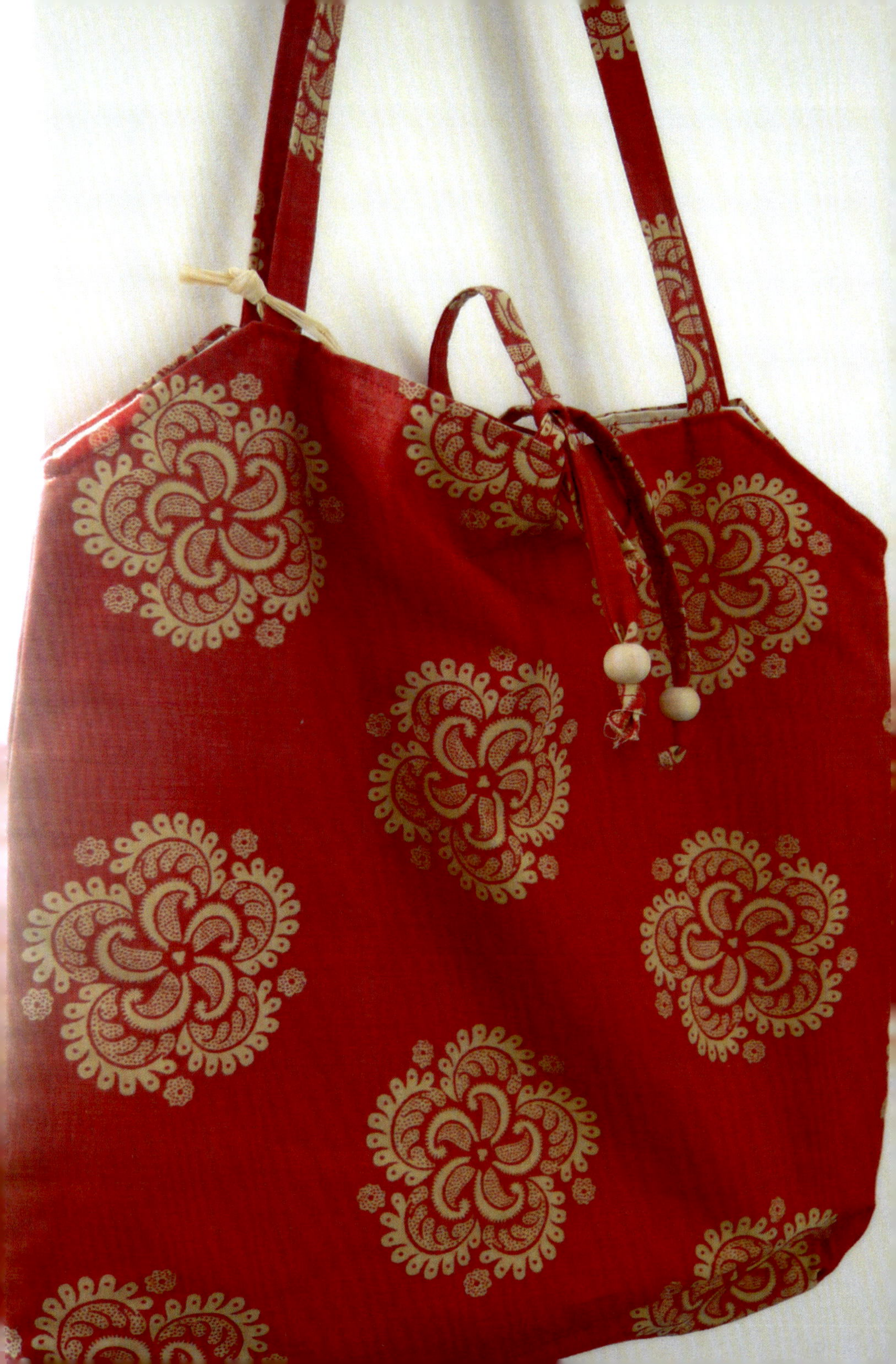

Shoulder Bag

You will need:

front/back: 2 pieces 35cm x 35cm (14" x 14")
base: 1 piece 10cm x 35cm (4" x 14")
straps: 2 pieces 4cm x 70cm (1 1/2" x 28")
ties: 2 pieces 3cm x 35cm (1" x 14")
lining fabric: 1 piece 35cm x 76cm (14" x 30")

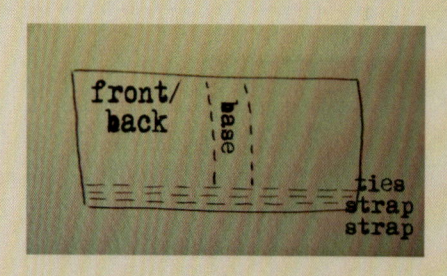

Take the long strip and fold the long edges into the middle so the raw edges meet. Fold in half again, pin and stitch close to the edge. Turn strip over and sew another line of stitching down the other side to strengthen. Repeat for other strap. Follow the same process for both ties

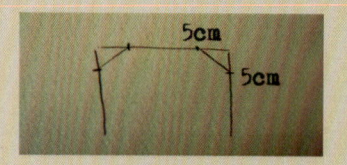

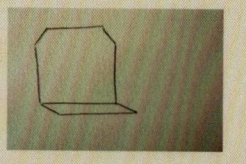

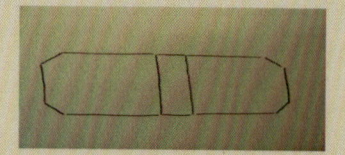

Measure 5cm (2") along the top edge and down each side Mark and cut out the triangle (this will be the top of the bag) With right sides together, attach the base to the bottom of one side, then join the other side.

With right sides together, sew down the side to join with the base. Zigzag fold the base and stitch on through to the end. Repeat on the other side.

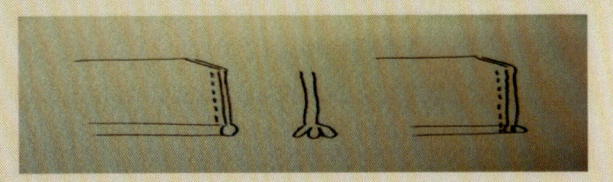

Fold the lining fabric in half with right sides together, and cut the triangles out same as for the outer fabric.
Sew down each side and then place lining into the outer bag.

Turn 1cm (1/2") in along the top edge on both the outer and lining and pin together adjusting if necessary

Pin straps and ties in position

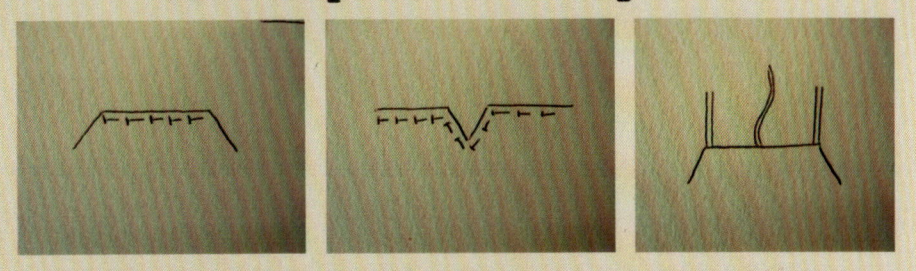

double check the straps are the same length and then stitch around the top of the bag. Over stitch the straps and ties to strengthen

Thread beads onto the ends of the ties and tie a knot to secure.

Baby Bear

You will need:
Mohair fabric for the head
Linen yarn/DK/wool for the body
Toy filler (UK = sc / US = DC)
small piece calico / dress fabric / ribbon

Use the pattern for the head/ears/nose from the Bear in a Box. Sew ears right side together, turn through, and sandwich between the head pieces and sew around. Turn to right side and stuff. Cut nose piece from calico, and sew features on nose piece, then sew a gathering stitch around the edge, put a small piece of toy filler in the inside and pull to gather and then sew in position on the front of face, then sew eyes on. Sew a gathering stitch around the bottom of the head, pull up and secure.

Body - crochet:
R1: 2ch, then 6 sc into chain nearest hook (6)
R2: 2sc into each stitch (12)
working in a spiral, 1 sc into each stitch until work measures 4cm (1 1/2") approx 60 stitches, cut yarn and finish, pull the ends of the yarn through to the inside of the body and stuff with toy filler
arms & legs
R1: 2ch then 4sc into chain nearest hook (4)
R2: 2 sc into each stitch (8)
working in spiral, 1 sc into each stitch until work measures 4cm (1 1/2") approx 45 stitches

Using sewing thread sew the top of the body to the head piece, then using the tail ends of the yarn from the arm and leg pieces sew to body.
Make your bear a dress (same pattern as for the Bear in a box)

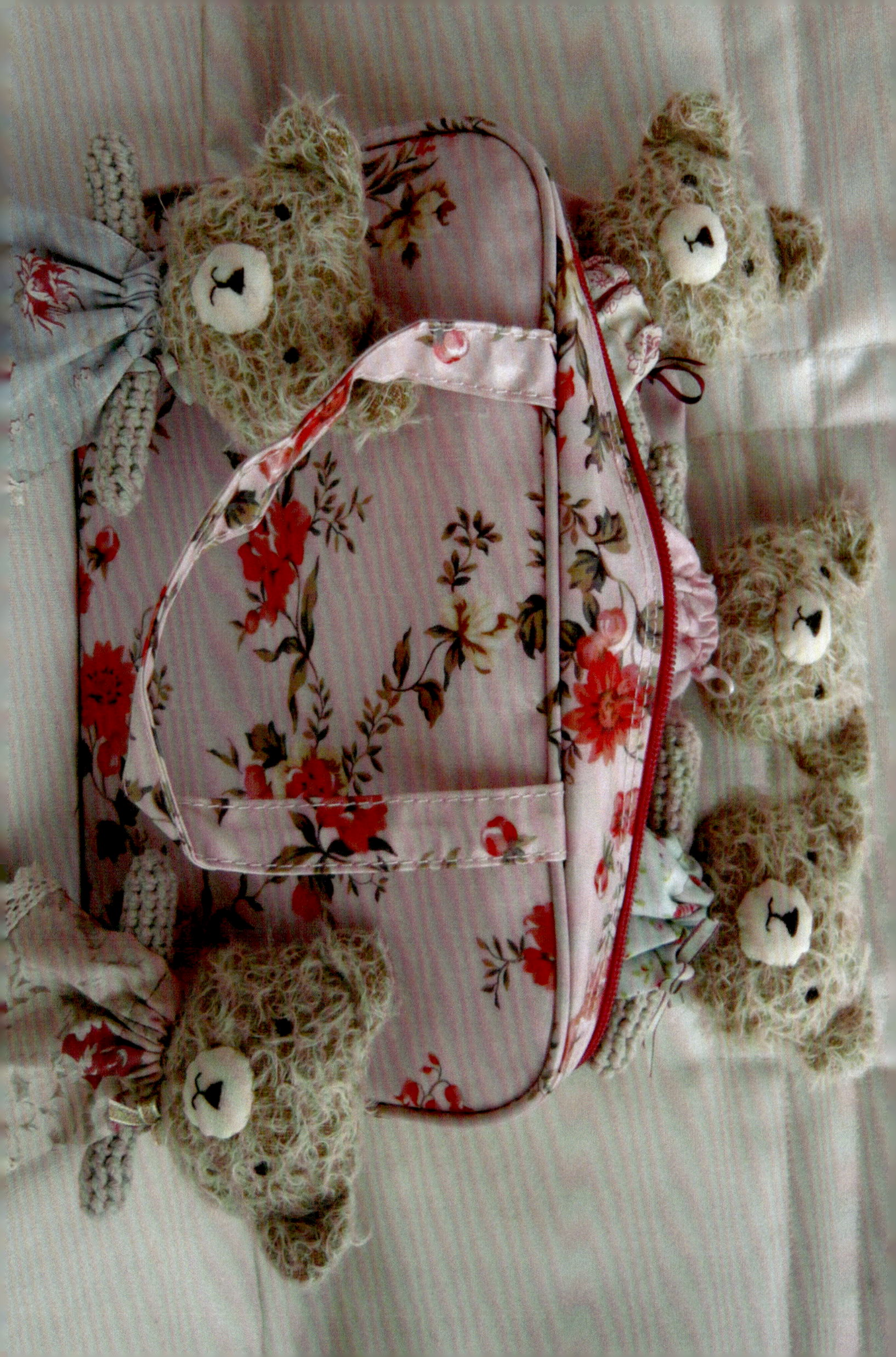

Country Girl Corner

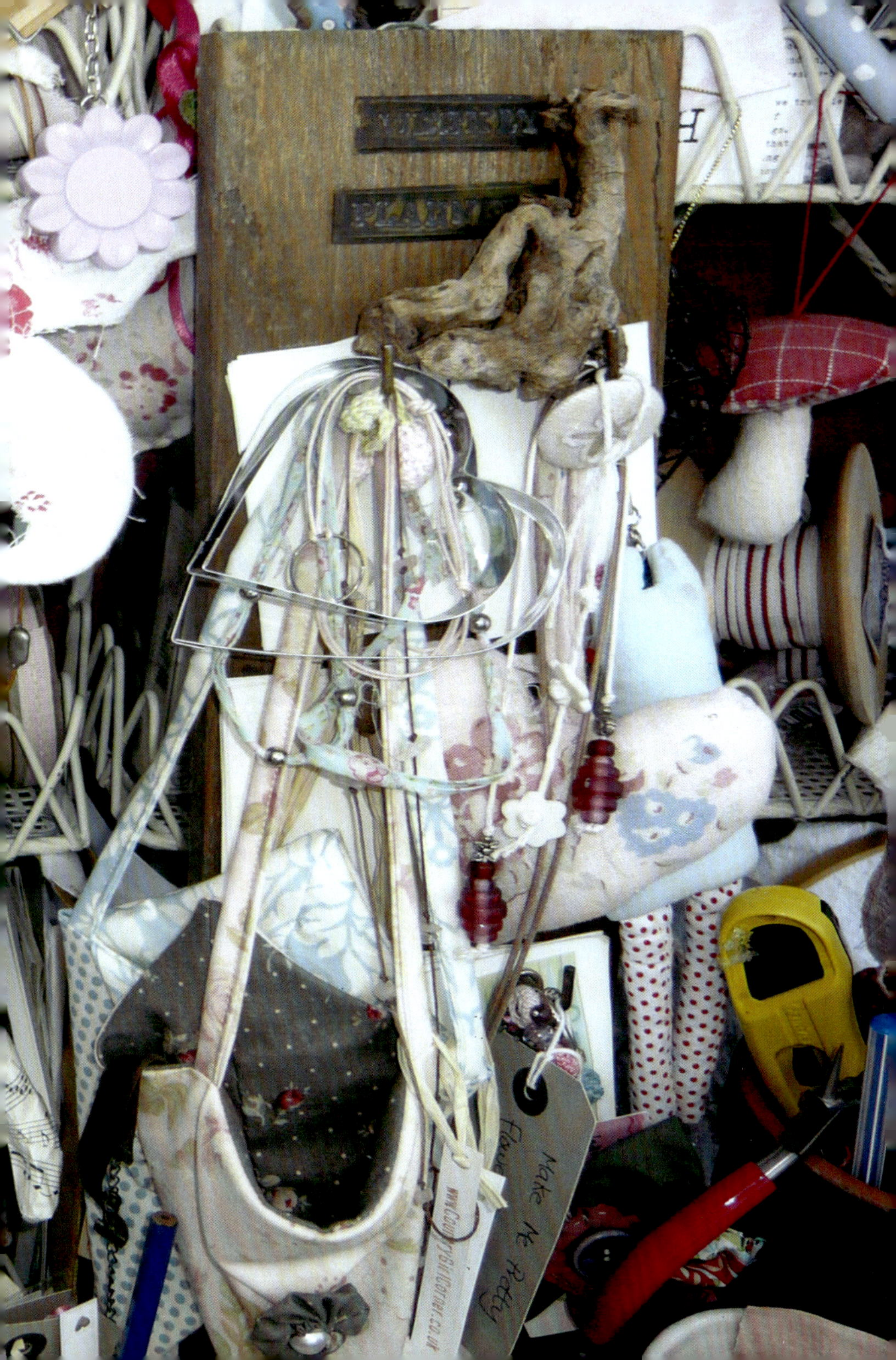
Make Me Pretty

A Very BIG Adventure

Having been making things for years and giving them as presents and subsequently supplying a few local shops, I decided I would apply to the Country Living Fair in the Design Centre, London. I checked out the details on-line, and printed out an application form and compiled a box of samples to be sent to the 'committee' who would decide whether my products were good enough to be accepted to join in the highly esteemed band of exhibitors at the biyearly show. This was about six weeks prior to the Spring show of that year, and they phoned me a few days later to say I'd been accepted and would I like to exhibit at the Spring Show. I was absolutely buzzing at the news, but there was absolutely no way I would have enough stock to be ready until the Christmas show. Everyone I spoke to said, make sure you have enough stock, one girl even said the first time she did it, she sold out on the first day and she sat for the remaining show not really knowing what to do, So, armed with the motto 'Be Prepared', I researched as much as I could about the show, and it was frightening!! You send off your application with a monster sized deposit and then wait, and wait.... and wait some more and then suddenly one day a large heavy package arrives. A thick A4 spiral bound book comes full of forms: forms for lighting, forms for layout, forms for insurance, forms for health and safety, forms for storage, get the picture there were a lot of forms. But as with all of these types of things, baby steps, one page at a time (keeping copies of everything, I got everything filled in and returned, and then sat back, and hmm waited some more.
(Did I mention I'd never even done a craft show before!)

While I was doing all the waiting, I was making, making loads of stuff, my room started to fill up. I tried to bag and tag as I went along, because surprisingly this is really time consuming, just tying a label on everything can take hours, and slowly things got counted and boxed. We were at car boots, street markets, charity shops, jumble sales, I hunted Ebay and Etsy looking for little bits of useful stuff which could be used in my ever growing list of products. I needed furniture for my stall (which was the smallest they offered 3msq), I figured I would need to display up the walls to make the most use of the space, so I had my Dad make me some hangable display boards for the lavender cats, we bought foldable shelf units and painted them French Grey, we found an old foldable table at the Ascot car boot, I had a baguette basket which was used for draught excluders, I had wooden towel rails for quilts, three pronged tea-towel hangers for lavender bags, anything I thought would be useful was brought home and put in the shed. Lucia and I had some fun one afternoon in the garden, I brought out the measuring tape and put markers in the grass, and then we laid out the various bits of furniture so I could get an idea of the scale we were working to, our cat Marvin was making full use of the activity in the garden, and it all fitted exactly the way I knew it would - I knew because I had been seeing it in my dreams and I had been visualising every square inch of the thing, so I knew it would work and how it would look, but I suppose you need to go through the motions to make sure.......

The day before the show, I filled my car and went to work. My husband filled his car and we met up at the venue and I started to unload while he painted the walls of the stand and stamped hearts randomly around and fitted a 'roof' to make it look more like a room. Then we assembled the furniture, fitted all the hanging and standing displays, and unpacked boxes and boxes of stock until the stand looked exactly how I'd imagined it would. We were knackered and went home exhausted. Next morning I was in the car first thing driving up to London, I checked the stand, adjusted a few things, turned on the lights and I was ready. Everyone around me was great fun, they had all done this a hundred times before so it was just like any other day at the office for them, but to me it was really new and exciting.

Then I heard it, the noise, it was like a great rumble getting louder and louder, for a moment I didn't realise what it was, and then a bell sounded, and it was the warning that the doors had opened and the great paying public were on their way. One of my first customers was a girl from Poland, she had arrived on an early flight with a huge empty suitcase, and started at one side of the stand and gathered armfuls of things, and happy with that, off she went. I saw her again about three hours later, hauling the suitcase behind her, whereupon she started at the other side of the stand and gathered more pictures and bears and off she went back to Poland content she had bought the best of the fair.

The five days went by so quickly, my friend Ange came down to help me on the stall and we had a really good laugh.

Some people made me really emotional, when they just stood in front of the stand with their mouths open and just admired and complimented everything and dug out cash from inside boots, and out of bras (where they had hidden money from themselves) and had looked at everything on offer, and had ecided that the thing on my stand was the one thing they really, really wanted. Throughout each day we would see people in the morning, and they would come back later on (we reckoned it would take three hours to look around, have a cup of tea, make decisions, and come back) and each night I went home exhausted. As each day went on, I realised there was one day less to go, and all the hard work for nearly a year was almost over. The breakdown day was difficult, everyone had to be out within a few hours, and everyone needed the lifts and the porters and there were queues for everything, but we plodded on, and eventually everything was dismantled and in the cars, and it was time to go home. Just as I was checking I hadn't left anything behind, a girl came round and handed out details for the next fair....................

I really enjoyed doing the show, there is an excitement which you don't get with the smaller shows and you'll be happy to know I had made enough stock (of most things). I had a lot of follow up enquiries from shops all over the place, a few people who were asking if I still had that thing...... and I know I'll do another one, when I've gathered my thoughts, topped up my energy and have a spare year to get ready!

Country Girl Corner

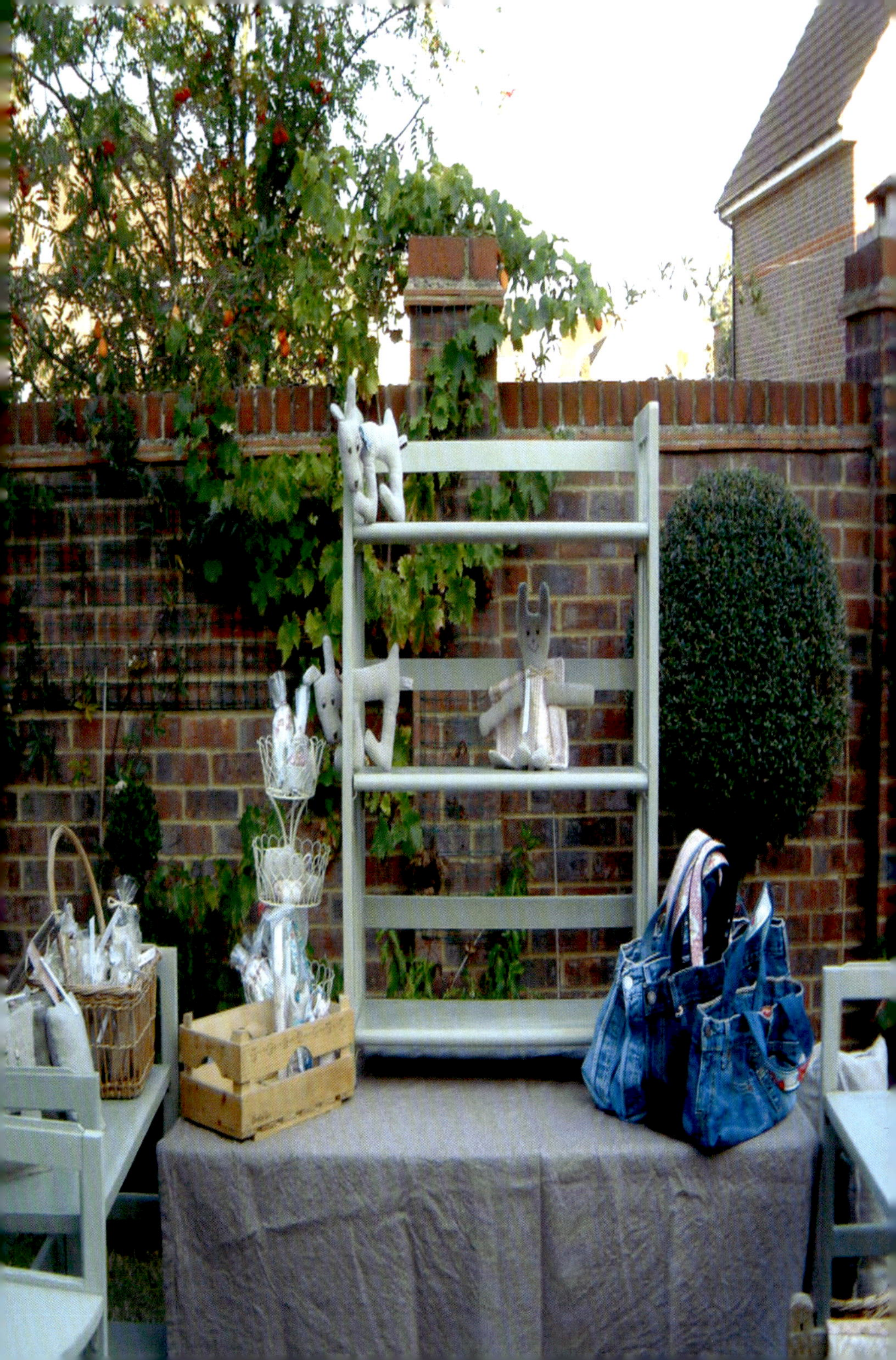

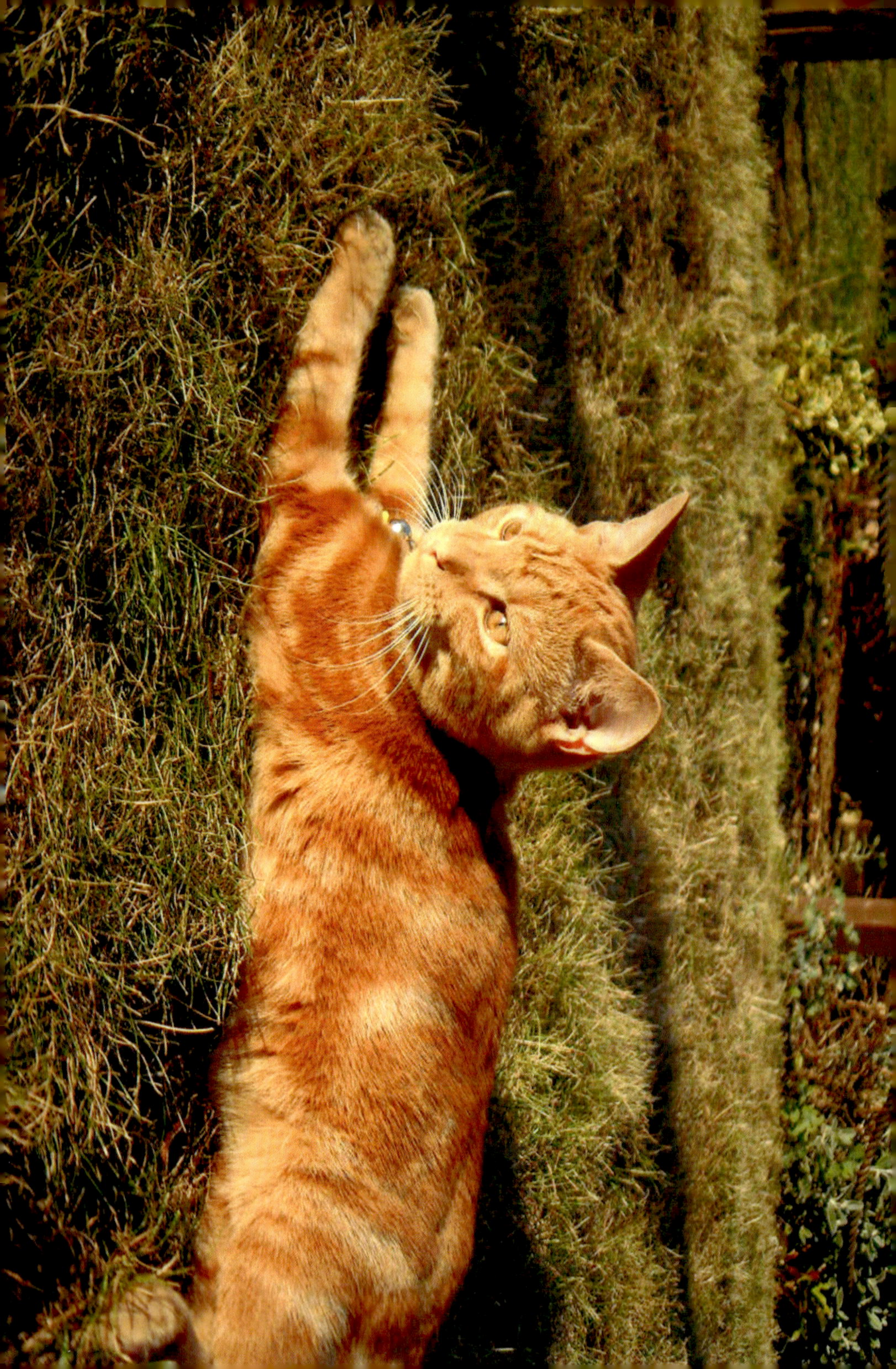

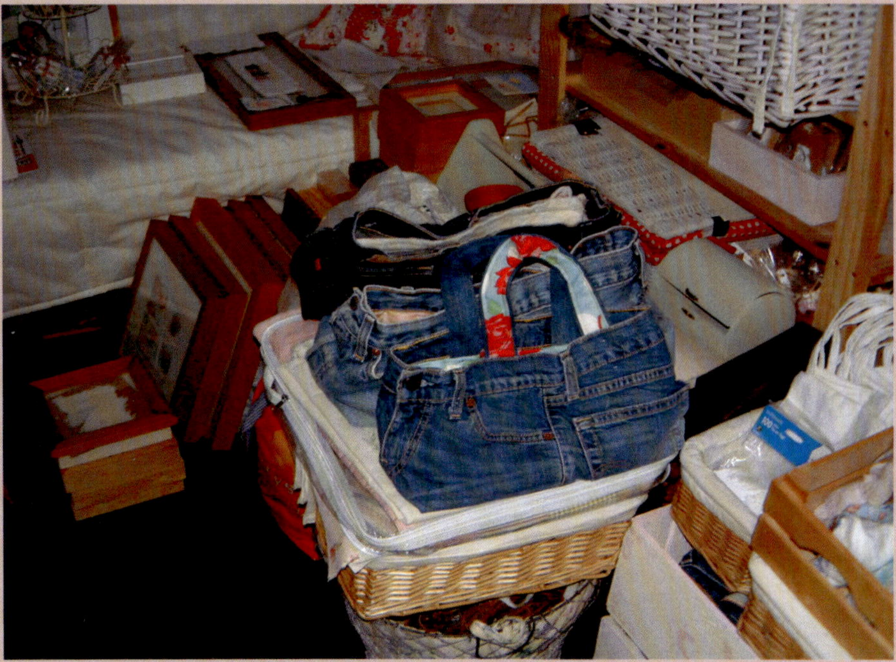

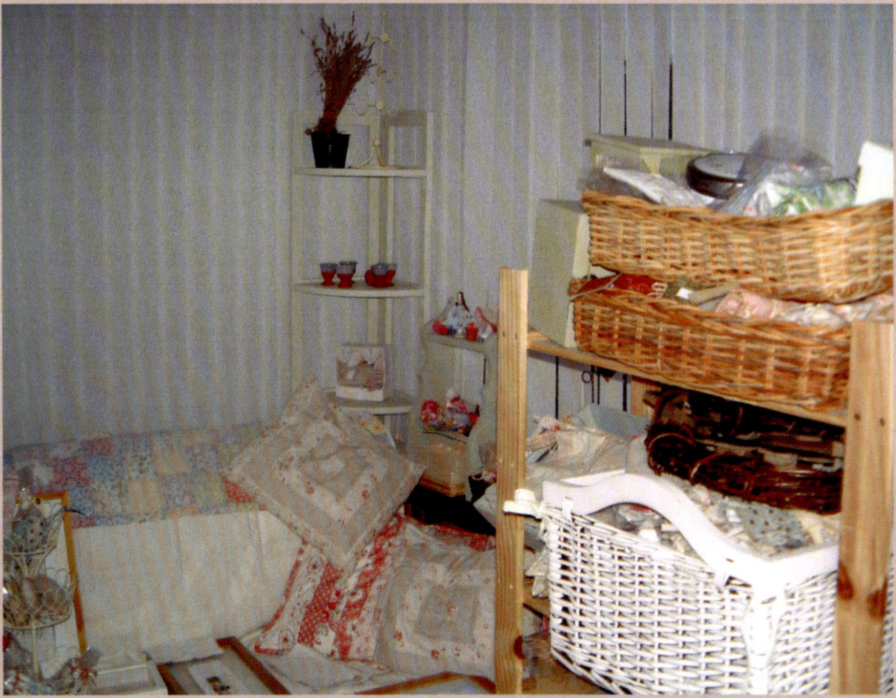

Pictures were framed, cats and dogs were put in boxes, bags were made, tags were stamped, miles of raffia was used, boxes were borrowed, paint was bought, every detail was thought of. I had even bought fabulous small plastic bags in the fish market in Setubal in Portugal when we were there on holidays and I had small brown paper bags (the type you get in green-grocers) and I had stamped Country Girl Corner along the top edge, I felt like I was ready!!

COUNTRY GIRL CORNER   T12

Country Girl Corner

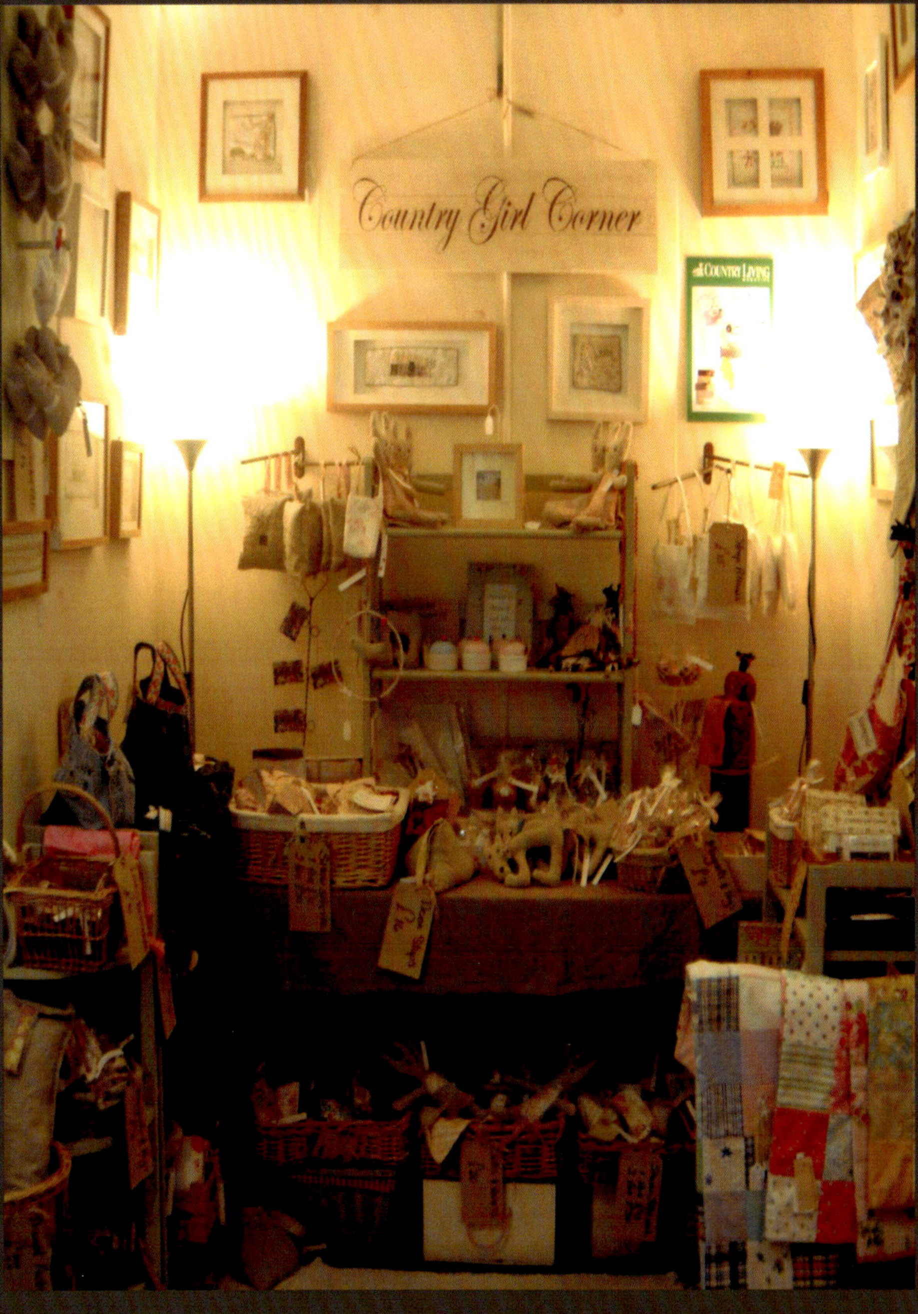
Country Girl Corner

ARTS, CRAFTS & ANTIQUES FAIR
SUNDAY – here at the Guildhall

LADIES

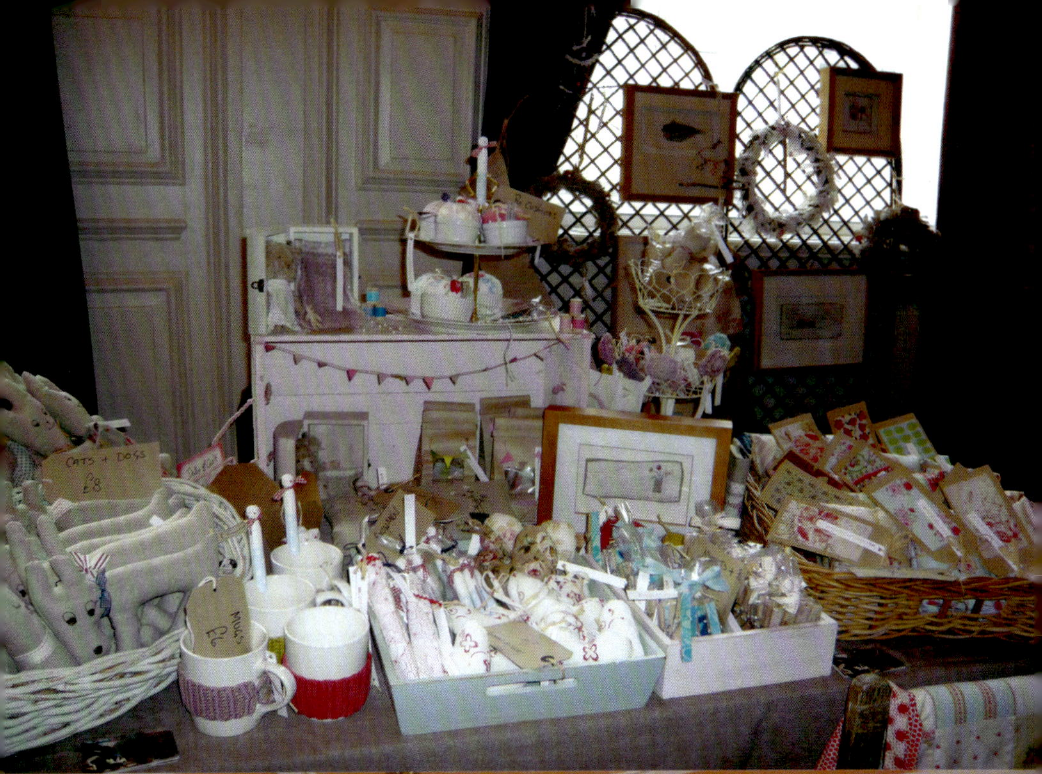
CATS + DOGS
£8
MUGS £6

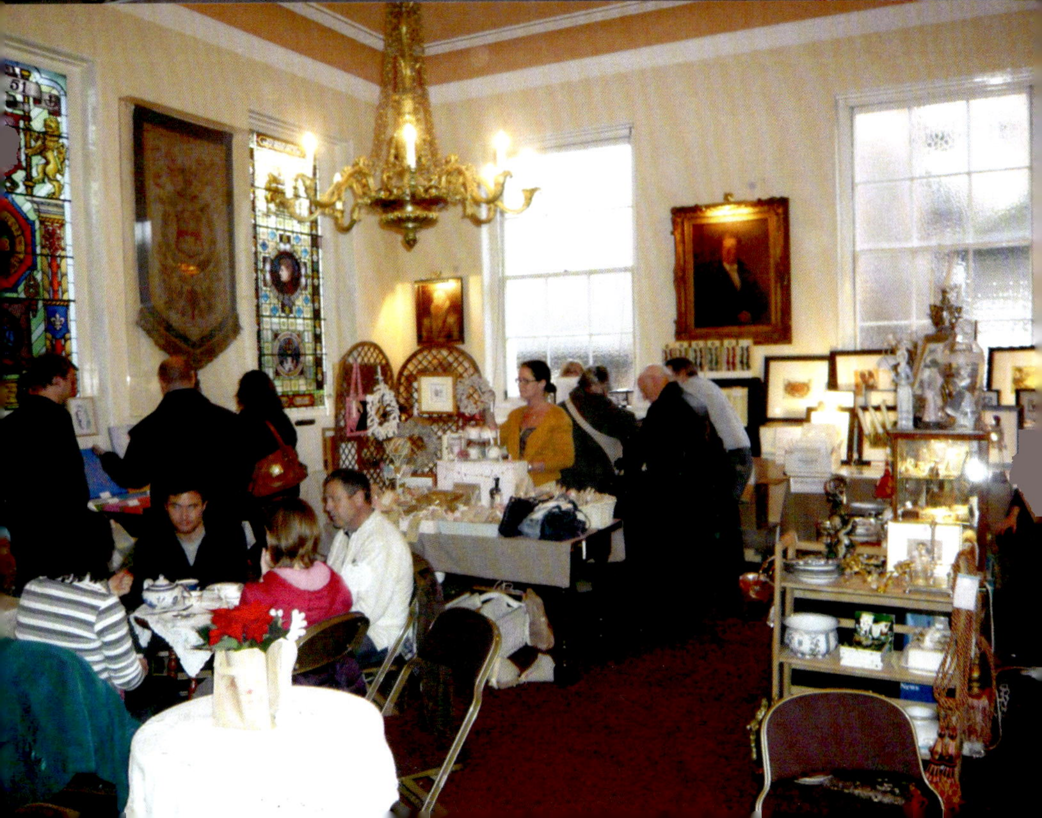

Gallery

Here are some pictures of various things I've made which are either further examples of items in the book, products which don't have patterns, new creations which I'm still working on, or are one-offs or commissions.

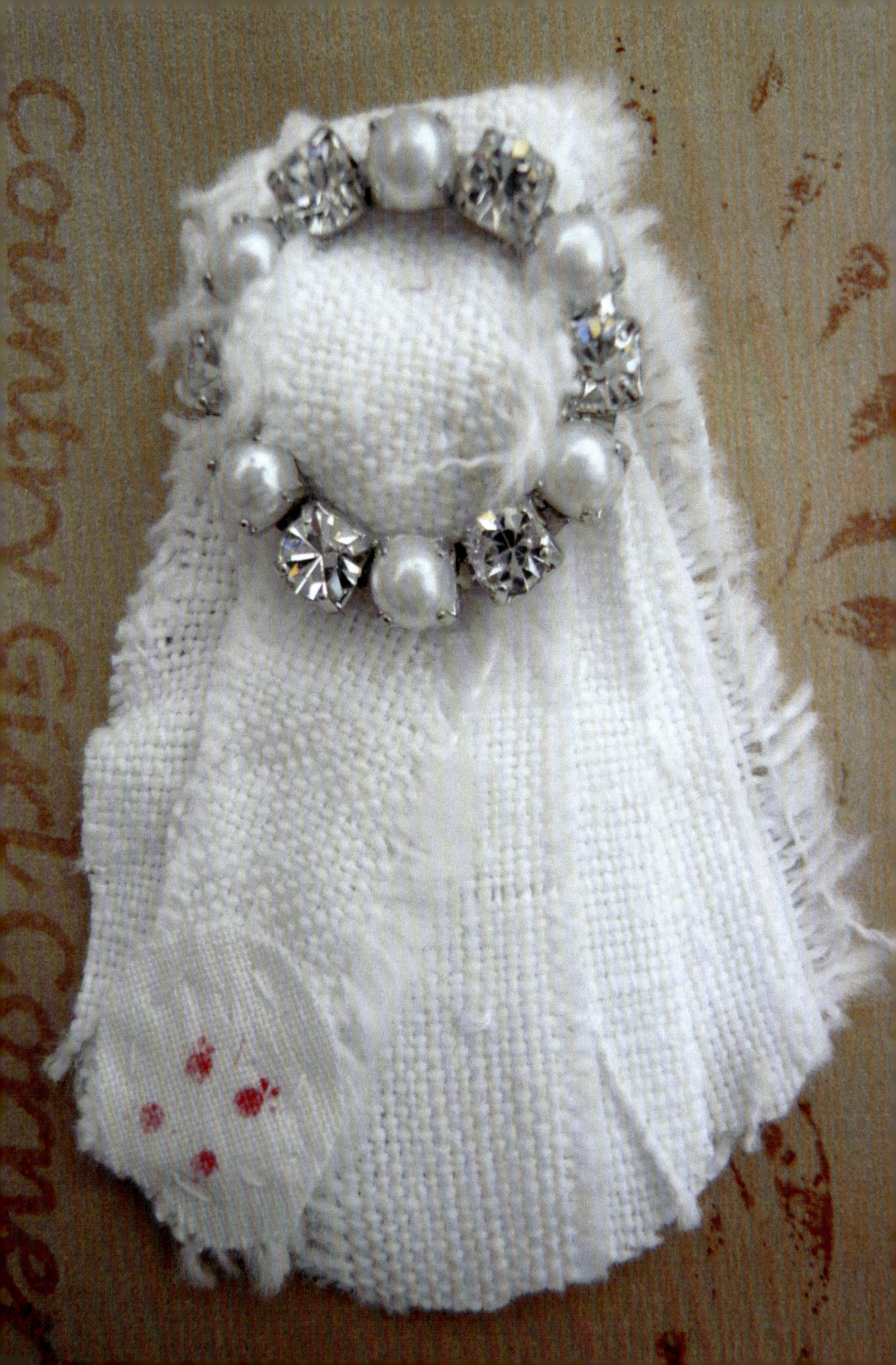

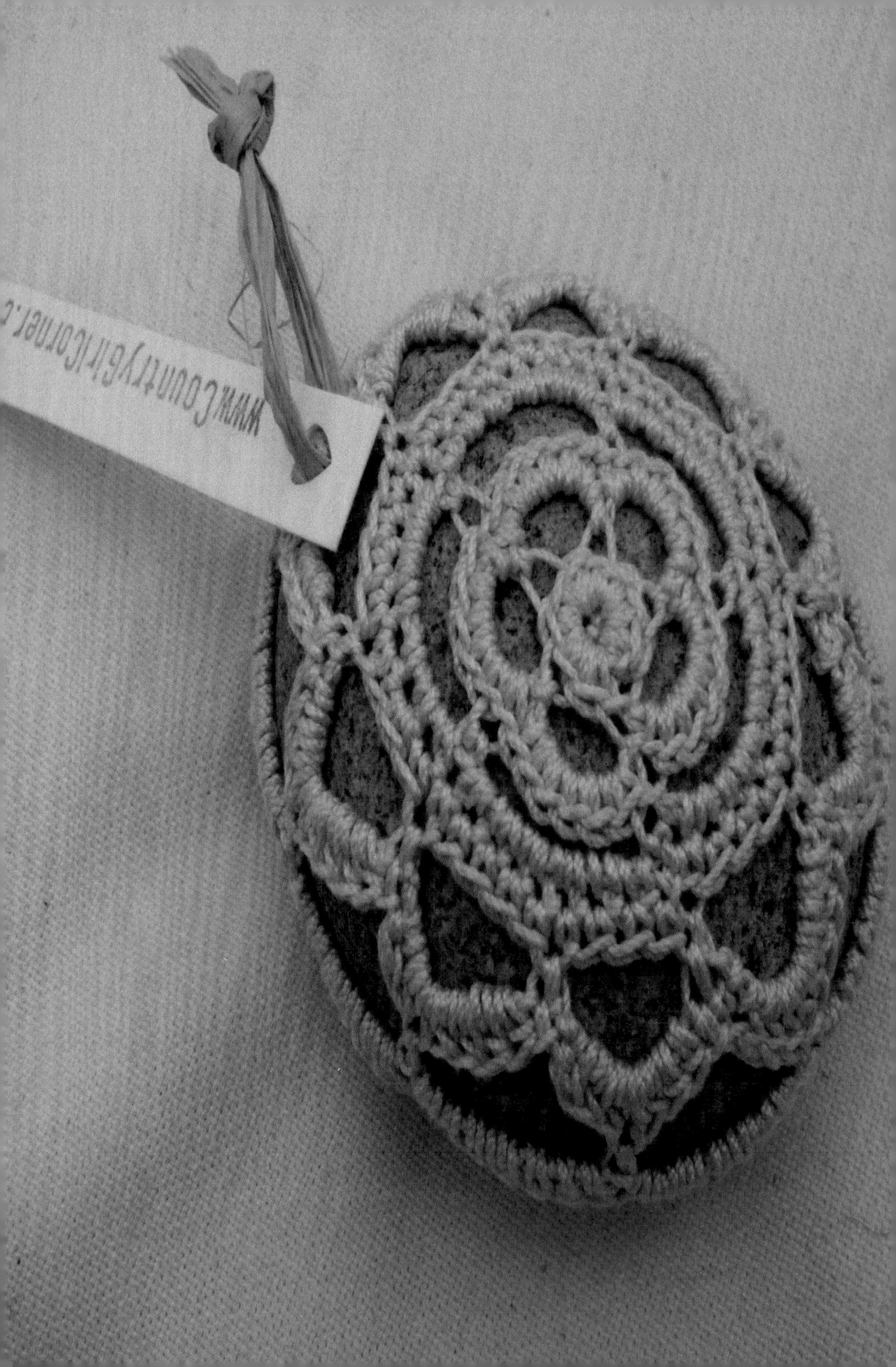
www.CountryGirlCorner.c

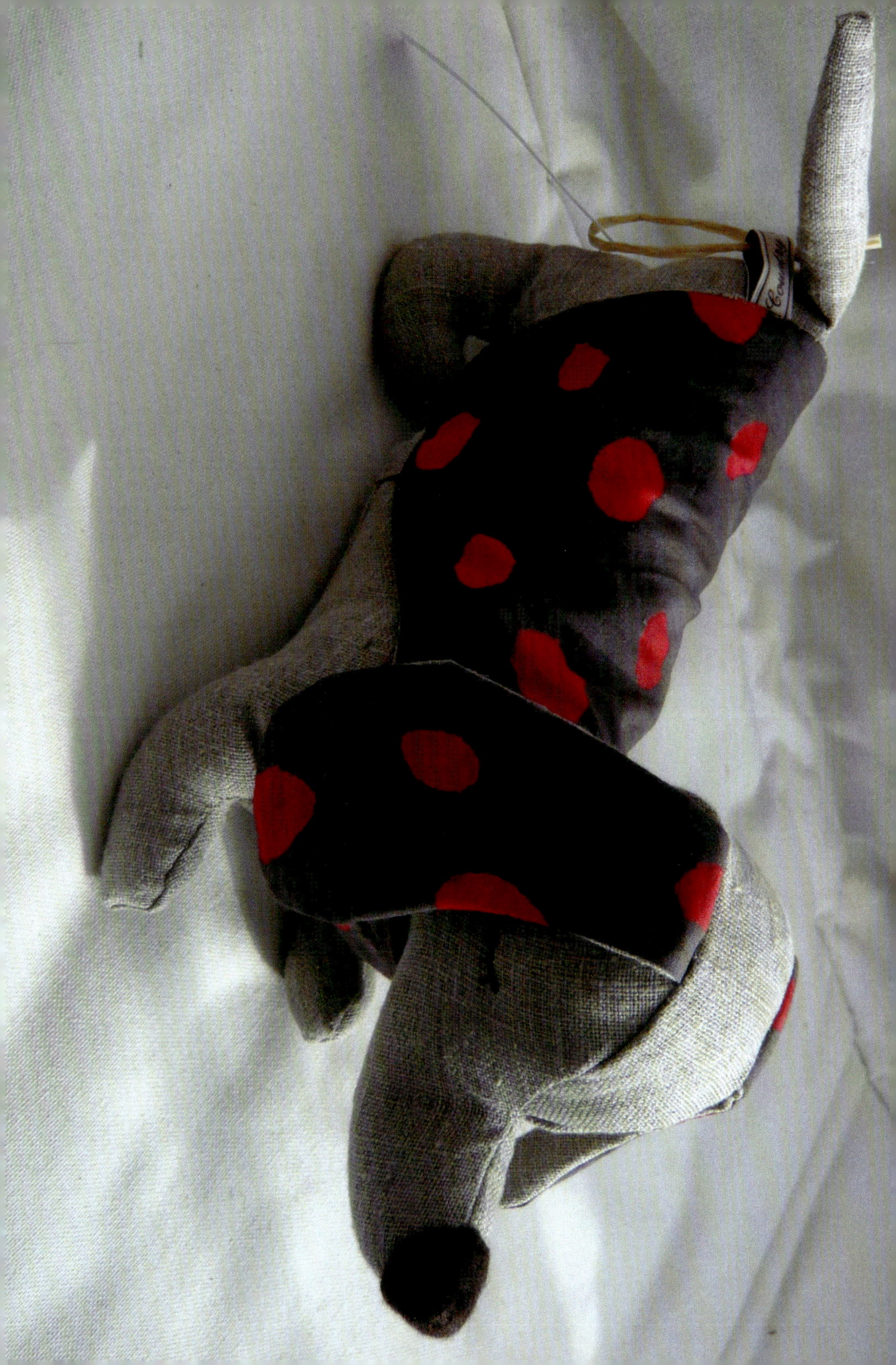

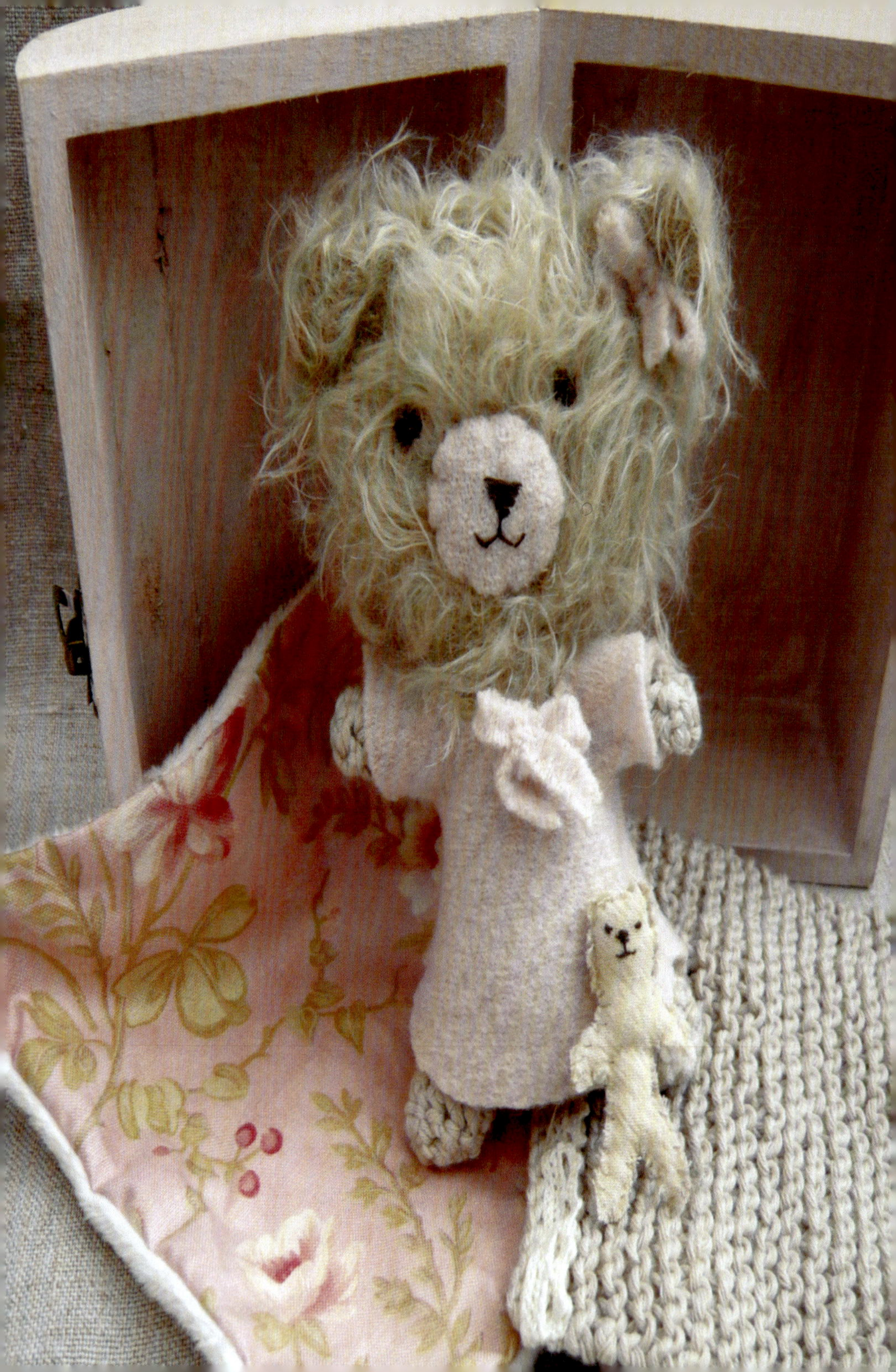

Lucio

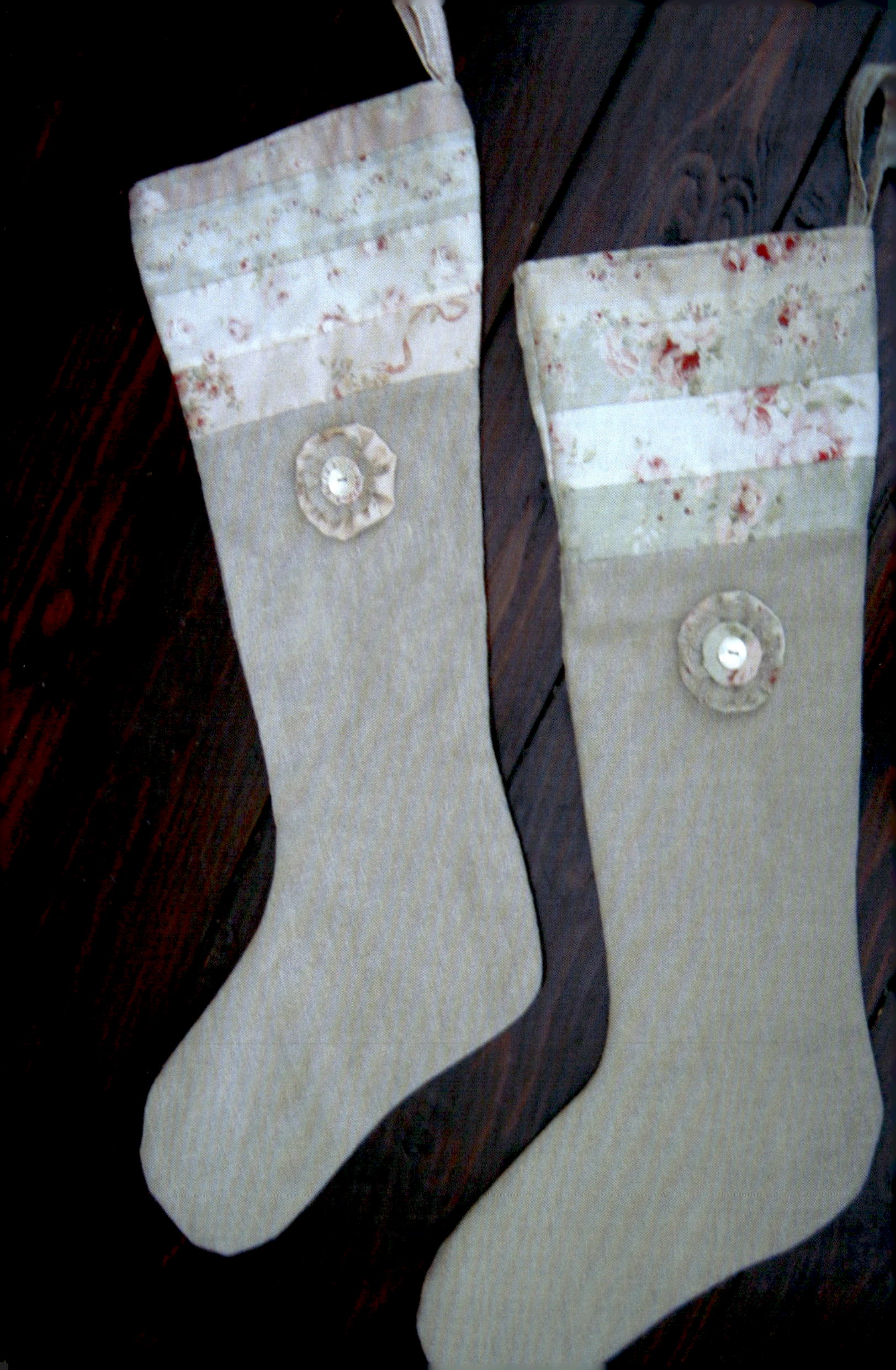

Computer bunting

Vintage button hair clips

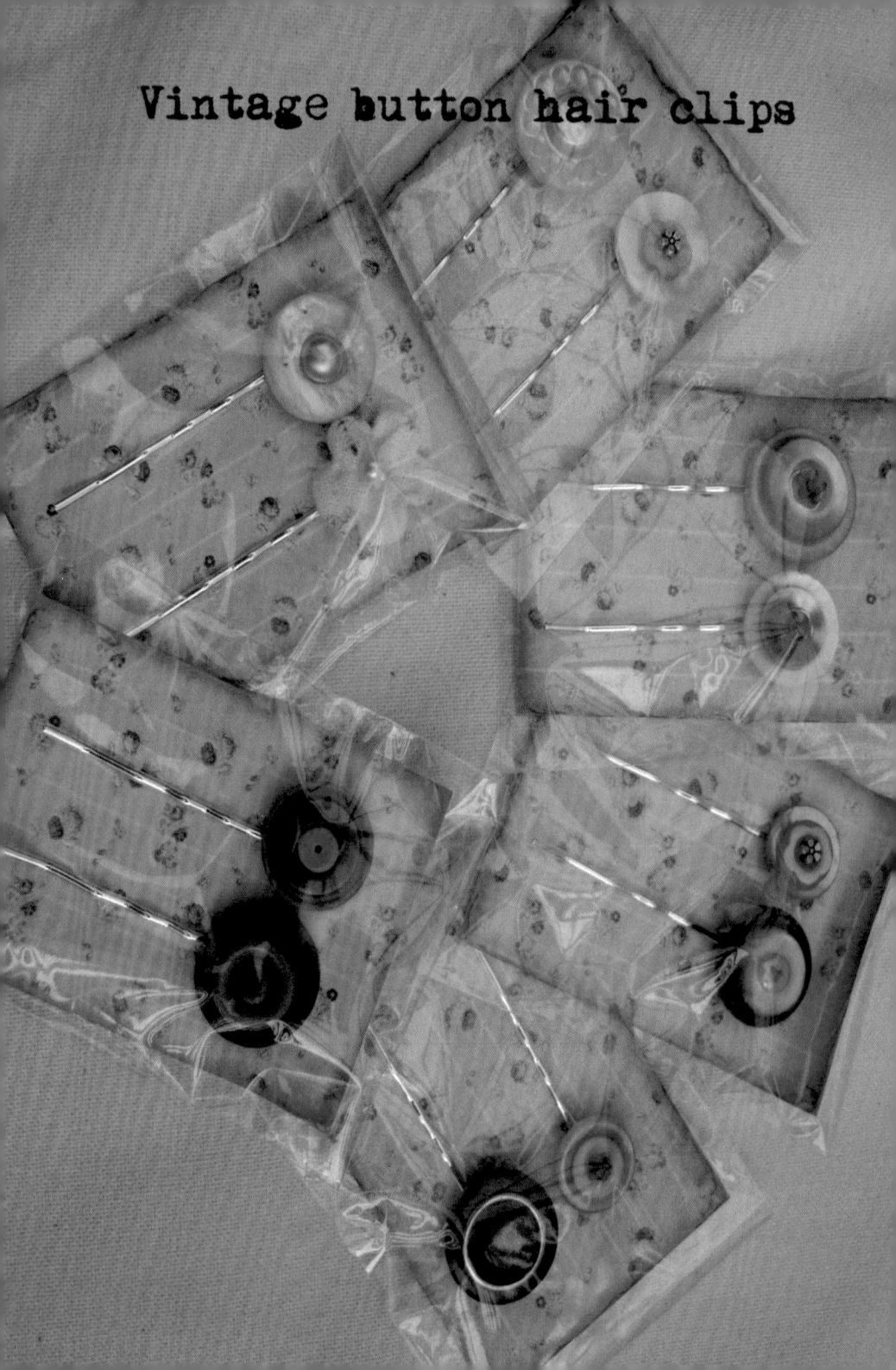

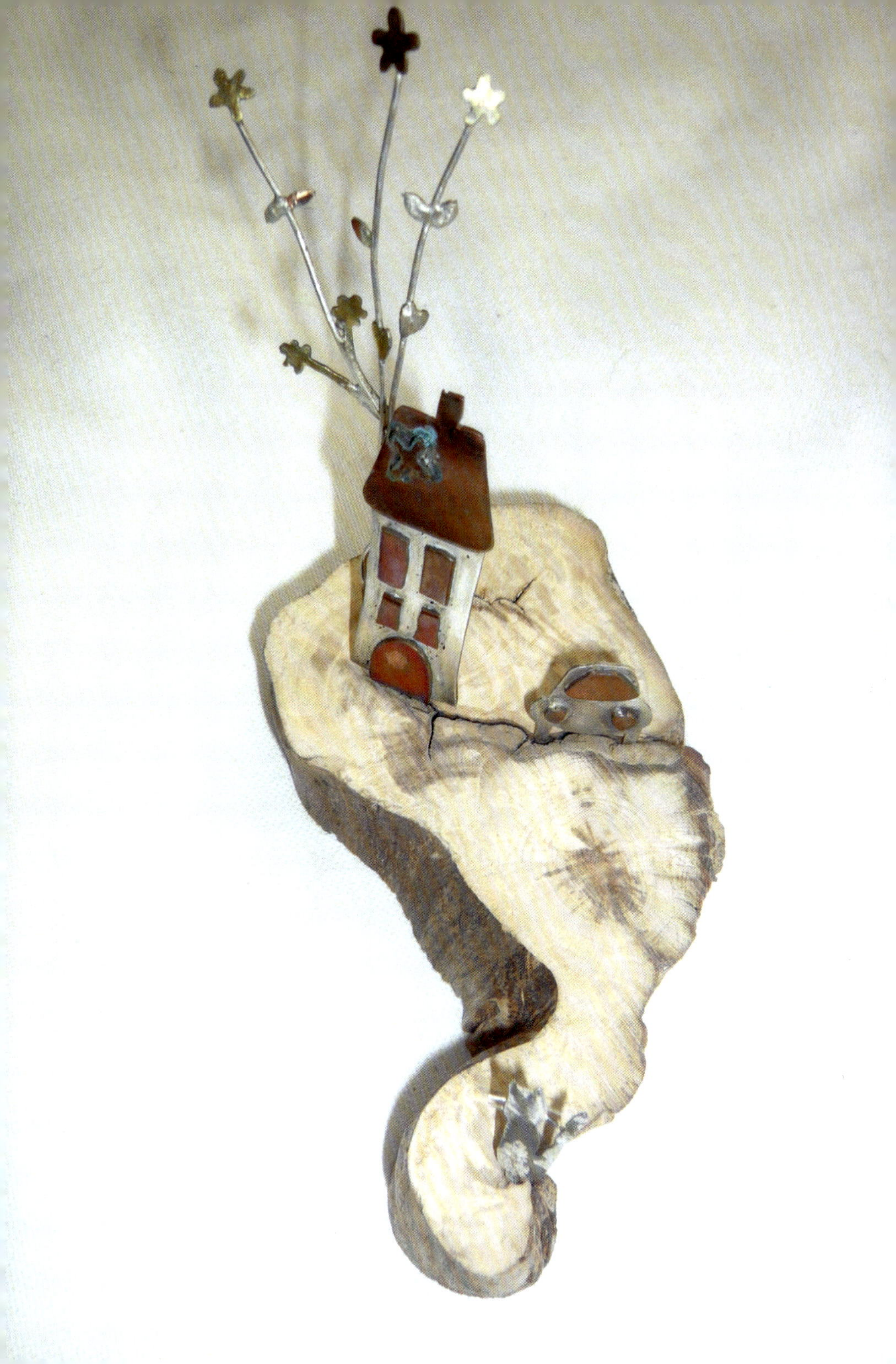

Row of Houses

'The Shay Car'

Lesley De Klerk

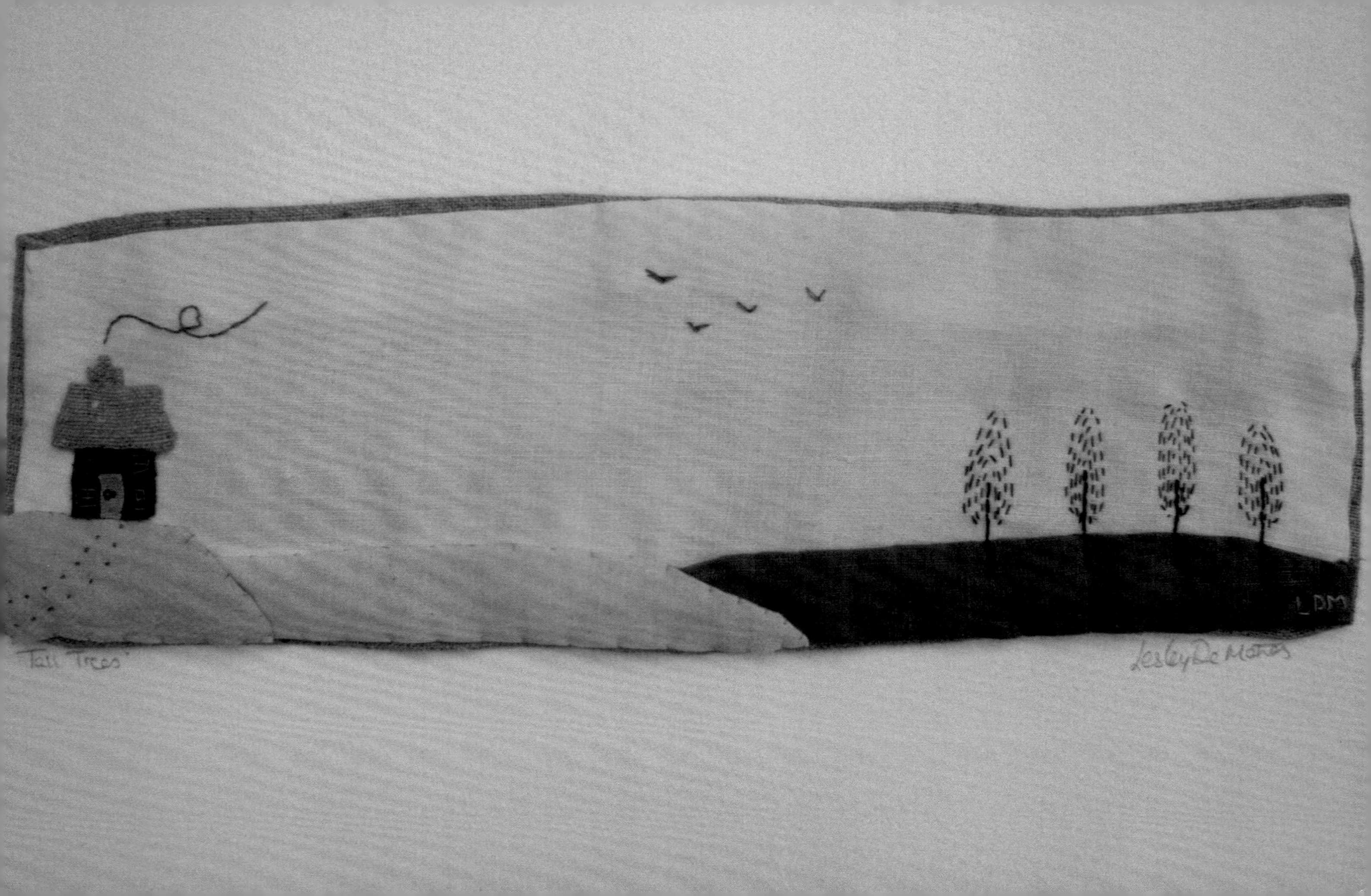
'Tall Trees'
LDM
Lesley De Mares

Index

3 Intro

5 From Typing to Photoshop

8 Missy the Lavender Cat

12 Buttons the Dog & Little Kittens

18 Quilt in a day

24 Stick leg doll

28 Hug in a rug

32 Bear in a box

36 Raggedy Anne

40 Rag wreaths

45 Lavender Hearts

46 Bird Mobile

50 Flowerpot Lavender Bags

56 Cupcake Pin Cushion

60 Lavender & wheat bag

64 Draught Excluder

68 Magnets & Pegs

72 Cushions

76 Lap Quilt

79 Fuzzy Brooch

82 Rose Quartz Bracelet

84 Liberty Bracelet

86 Spring Rose Brooch

90 Button necklace

92 Pearl necklace

94 Amethyst lariat

96 Activity Bag

100 Denim Bag

106 Notebook Cover

110 Shoulder Bag

114 Baby Bear

118 - 129 Country Living

130 Windsor Emporium

132 Gallery

146 Index

148 Credits

149 CD-ROM

Thanks to Krys Evans and Alex Adams who have always supported my creations and given me opportunities, goodies and support just when I really needed them.

Thanks to Bert Dufour who programmed my CD-ROM to work beautifully.
www.dufour.me.uk

Thank you to Dan (www.dancorbett.co.uk) who provided all the technical support and answered all my questions about Photoshop

Also thanks to some fabulous people from Etsy:

Onelittlepenguin
Pastelstrawberry